China's Economic Refor

China's growth miracle over the past 30 years has propelled it to become the world's second largest economy and potentially the largest in the following years. This book examines China's experience on economic reform, trying to find the reasons for the sustainable and rapid development and provide insights into the study of economic theories.

From the perspective of political economics, this book elaborates on China's socialist market economy, which was officially confirmed as the goal of the country's economic reform in 1992. It expounds on China's economic model, the relationship between socialism and market economy, as well as the establishment and improvement of socialist market economy in China, deepening the studies in the laws governing China's economic development. Then, it explores the gradual reform, the reform of state-owned enterprises and the relationship between governments and market, all of which are crucial to the success of China's economic reform. Finally, based on the earlier analysis, this book discusses the reasons for the constant and rapid development of China's economy.

With detailed analysis on the Reform experience and theoretical implications, this book will appeal to scholars and students studying China's economy, and contribute to the development of economic theories.

Yu Zhang is Professor of economics at Renmin University of China, one of China's top universities for economics. He has been devoted to the studies of political economics and socialist market economy for more than 20 years.

China Perspectives

The *China Perspectives* series focuses on translating and publishing works by leading Chinese scholars, writing about both global topics and China-related themes. It covers Humanities and Social Sciences, Education, Media and Psychology, as well as many interdisciplinary themes.

This is the first time any of these books have been published in English for international readers. The series aims to put forward a Chinese perspective, give insights into cutting-edge academic thinking in China, and inspire researchers globally.

For more information, please visit www.routledge.com/series/CPH

Existing titles in economics

Internet Finance in China
Introduction and Practical Approaches
Ping Xie, Chuanwei Zou, Haier Liu

Regulating China's Shadow Banks
Qingmin Yan, Jianhua Li

Internationalization of the RMB
Establishment and Development of RMB Offshore Markets
International Monetary Institute of the RUC

The Road Leading to the Market
Weiying Zhang

Peer-to-Peer Lending with Chinese Characteristics
Development, Regulation and Outlook
P2P Research Group Shanghai Finance Institute

Forthcoming titles in economics

Tax Reform and Policy in China
Gao Peiyong

China Economic Transition Research
Zhao Renwei

China's Economic Reform

Experience and Implications

Yu Zhang

First published in English 2018
by Routledge

2 Park Square, Milton Park, Abingdon, Oxfordshire OX14 4RN
52 Vanderbilt Avenue, New York, NY 10017

Routledge is an imprint of the Taylor & Francis Group, an informa business

First issued in paperback 2020

Translated by Hang Jiang

Published in Chinese by China Renmin University Press, 2015

British Library Cataloguing-in-Publication Data
A catalogue record for this book is available from the British Library

Library of Congress Cataloging-in-Publication Data
Names: Zhang, Yu, 1964 January– author.
Title: China's economic reform : experience and implications / Yu Zhang.
Description: Abingdon, Oxon ; New York, NY : Routledge, 2018. | Series:
    China perspectives | Includes index.
Identifiers: LCCN 2017030212 | ISBN 9781138089082 (hardcover) |
    ISBN 9781315109459 (ebook)
Subjects: LCSH: China—Economic policy—1949– | China—Economic
    conditions—1949–
Classification: LCC HC427.95 Z43547 2018 | DDC 330.951—dc23
LC record available at https://lccn.loc.gov/2017030212

ISBN: 978-1-138-08908-2 (hbk)
ISBN: 978-0-367-53441-7 (pbk)

Typeset in Times New Roman
by Apex CoVantage, LLC

Contents

1 Practices of economic reform and development of economics in China

Since the Third Plenary Session of the 11th Central Committee of the Communist Party of China, on the basis of achievements made in revolution and construction after the foundation of the New China, China has successfully explored the new road for socialist economic development with Chinese characteristics. As the Chinese economy has attracted all eyes worldwide for its vigorous vitality and vigor, China's Model, China's Experiences and China's Road have become the focus of attention of the whole world. It is a significant and urgent task of the current age for Chinese economics circle to correctly summarize the great practices of Reform and Opening Up in China, establish the economics system and academic discourse system with Chinese characteristics, Chinese style and Chinese manner and enhance consciousness and confidence of economics in China.

I. Promote the development of theories based on practices

Theory reflects practices. Closely linked with practices of the construction of socialist economy with Chinese characteristics, contemporary economics of China, on the one hand, profoundly reflects the historical course and practice requirements of Reform and Opening Up and economic development in China, and, on the other hand, renders theoretical support for it in China and promotes development of practices.

In the early days after the foundation of the New China, directed against economic construction indiscriminately imitating the pattern of the Soviet Union at that time, Mao Zedong put forward that "the communist party and the circle of intellectuals of each country shall create new theories, write new works and produce their own theorists to serve current politics, instead of merely relying on ancestors".[1] He called on the whole Party to learn from experiences and lessons of the Soviet Union and pushed forward the "second combination" of Marxism-Leninism and practical conditions of China. To this end, he had written important documents on guiding economic construction, including *On the Ten Major Relationships* and *Draft of Sixty Working Methods*, and tried to explore the road of socialist construction unique to China. He also suggested cadres of the whole party read *Socialist Economic Problems of the Soviet Union* written by Stalin several times and the "socialism part" in the third edition of *Teaching Material on Politics and Economics* prepared by the Institute of Economics of Soviet Union Academy of Sciences, which emphasized, "It is of great theoretical significance and practical significance to research on issues of politics and economics", explored on a series of major issues in socialist politics and economics and proposed many valuable thoughts and important ideas. For example, political work makes the lifeblood of all economic work; take agriculture as the base and industry as the guidance and guarantee coordinated development of agriculture and light and heavy industry; prepare overall plans, take all factors into consideration, make appropriate arrangement and attach importance to comprehensive balance; simultaneously focus on central and local work and give full play to initiative of the both; handle relationships among the country, collective and individual well, and enable them to be in their proper place; eliminate polarization and ultimately achieve common prosperity; see the value rule as a great school as well as a useful tool for socialist construction; "march toward science" and "implement technological revolution" to fully realize modern agriculture, industry, national defense and science and technology; and rely mainly on our own efforts while seeking assistance abroad. These thoughts and ideas have made important contributions to the development of socialist political economics in China.

Since the time of Reform and Opening Up, Chinese economy and society have been exposed to profound changes and rapid development; it attained rare development miracles along human history, made historical contributions to world development and provided extremely typical and rich materials for the development of contemporary economics. Meanwhile, China is a big socialist country with vast territory, a large population and time-honored tradition that is going through development and transformation. Encountered with the concurrence of several major historical changes such as industrialization, informatization, marketization, globalization and reform of socialist systems, China's practices and road are much more complicated, rich and special than those of any other country. As great practices are calling for theoretical innovation, the economics of China embraces unprecedented historical opportunities. As pointed out by Xi Jinping,

> Practice is the source for theories. China has gone through magnificent course and acquired great achievements that strike the attention of the world during its economic development, and has brought about the great driving force, vigor and potentiality to theoretical creation. We shall conduct profound study on global economy and new conditions and issues in Chinese economy, to contribute Chinese wisdom to innovation and development of Marxism Political Economics.[2]

In view of vigorous reform and development, since the Third Plenary Session of the 11th Central Committee of the Communist Party of China, the Communist Party of China has combined basic principles of Marxism and new practices in Reform and Opening Up and thus created the socialist political economics with Chinese characteristics. In October 1984, when the *Resolution of the Central Committee of the Communist Party of China on Economic System Reform* was approved, Deng Xiaoping praised this decision: "It has completed the first draft of political economics, the political economics that combine basic principles of Marxism and socialist practices in China".[3]

In the recent 30 years, socialist political economics with Chinese characteristics have made great progress along with vigorous development of practices and initially established the complete theoretical system, where the major theoretical ideas include the following: the essence of socialism is liberation and development of the productive forces, the elimination of exploitation and polarization, and the ultimate achievement of prosperity for all; the basic system at the primary stage of socialism is keeping public ownership as the mainstay of the economy and allowing diverse forms of ownership to develop side by side; the socialist market economy is the market economics integrating basic socialist system and market economy, which gives full play to advantages of both the market economy and socialist system; adhere to the system in which distribution according to work is dominant and a variety of modes of distribution coexist and combine efficiency improvement and equity promotion; actively participate in economic globalization and meanwhile insist on independence, to make good use of the two markets and two resources, respectively, in China and overseas; hold on to the people-oriented development idea and firmly establish the innovative, coordinated, green, open and shared development principles; and persist in the road of mutual coordination, favorable interaction and profound integration of new paths of industrialization, informatization, urbanization and agricultural modernization with Chinese characteristics and so on. These theoretical achievements constitute the political economics adapting to contemporary China's actual conditions and characteristics of the times, the new achievements of Chinization and modernization of Marxism political economics.

During this period, people in economic theory and academic circles gradually get rid of restrictions imposed by traditional theories of planned economy and transfer the focus of theories to the analysis of the practical course of economic operation as well as research and discussion on major issues in reform and development. The economics of China ushers in prosperous development. In terms of relations between theories and practices, achievements in economic research in China since Reform and Opening Up could be divided into three levels:

The first level is the research on countermeasures, such as investigation and research reports, and reform programs on macro-control system reform, enterprise reform, financial reform, fiscal reform, price reform, exchange rate reform, income distribution system reform and labor and social security system reform, as well as countermeasure reports and policy suggestions on national economic development plan, macro-economic policies and administrative measures for economy, etc. As for the theoretical structure, these researches belong to countermeasure research on the surface, which is closer to practical economic issues and further to basic economic theories. However, its significance cannot be underestimated, since it not only provides first-hand materials and references to economic decision-making by the Party and government but also renders important raw materials for development and innovation of economics in China. For instance, major theories and policies such as the application of the contract responsibility system, establishment of modern enterprise system of state-owned enterprises and proposal of indigenous innovation policy are all derived from researches on countermeasures.

The second level refers to researches on the basic theories of economic reform and economic development in China, such as discussions on productive forces and production relations, purpose of socialist production, economic effect, distribution on the basis of labor, relation between planned and market economy and rural land ownership in early 1980s; discussions on socialist planned commodity economy, economic operational mechanism and operational mode, whole thinking about economic reform and relation between inflation and economic growth, etc., in mid-1980s; discussions on essence and characteristics of socialist market economy, status and role of state-owned economy, content and form of modern enterprise system, relation between distribution on the basis of labor and distribution on the basis of production factors and essence and effect of economic globalization, etc., in the 1990s; and discussions on the train of thought to improve socialist market economy system, relation between efficiency and equity, new path of industrialization, third industrial revolution, relation between government and market, China's mode and China's path and theoretical system and academic discourse system of economics in China, etc., in the new century. These researches have promoted people's understanding about the laws of economic reform and development in China and the development of socialist economic theories with Chinese characteristics.

The third level is the research on general theories of economics, such as researches on economic methodologies, value theories, currency theories, enterprise theories, growth theories and crisis theories, etc. Though looking abstract and less related to practical economy, these researches play a significant role in scientifically understanding laws of economic development and formulating correct economic policies. For example, in the theoretical realm, the discussions on deepening the labor and labor theory of value center on how to understand the establishment of autonomy of Chinese enterprises in socialist market economy, the generation of pricing mechanism and reform of income distribution system; the discussions on ownership and enterprises theories center on how to solve theoretical foundation for governance structure and system design of state-owned enterprises, and discussions on the essence of contemporary capitalist economy and development trend are directly related to how to understand the international environment and historical orientation of socialism with Chinese characteristics and how to formulate the correct strategies on opening.

In conclusion, great achievements have been made in all those three levels of researches, which have promoted the development of economics theories in China and made significant contributions to practices of Reform and Opening Up. These achievements cannot be denied.

There is no need for reticence that economics of China is immature in general. Academic researchers are exposed to weak theories of foundation, copies of western economics and being unreliable, void and fickle, while the researches and academic innovation in economic theories evidently fall behind requirements proposed by practices and ages. This is normal in a certain sense. "Thoughts on form of life of human and then the scientific analysis always apply the road contrary to practical development. Thinking starts after the thing happens, which means starts from the results after completion of development course".[4] It is impossible for us to acquire mature and perfect theories of socialist economy before completion of socialist modernization construction in China. However, as long as we stick to correct direction, take the practices in China as a basis, take into consideration the Chinese history, confront bravely problems of China and summarize experiences, construct discourse, refine ideas and make innovation on theories, we can make theoretical achievements live up to the age and people and contribute more to human development.

II.   Adhere to Marxism as guidance

The primary task for the construction of economics of China lies in adhering to and developing Marxism political economics or economics and promoting Chinization and modernization of Marxism economics. Lenin once pointed out that political economics "are the most profound, comprehensive and detailed demonstration and application of Marxist theories". Engels once mentioned that the proletarian party has "all theories come from researches on political economics". During socialist economic construction with Chinese characteristics, Marxism economics play a special, significant and irreplaceable role.

(1) Scientific world outlook and methodology. The scientific nature of Marxist political economics is first reflected by its scientific world outlook – i.e., dialectical materialism and historical materialism. Based on the foundation of the outlook of dialectical materialism and historical materialism, Marxist economics also form the scientific methodology on analysis of economic phenomena, including the principle that productivity determines production relations and the economic base determines the superstructure, principle of analyzing individual economic behavior in the overall control of social and economic structure formed in the history, principle of determining the nature of the whole social and economic system based on the ownership of the means of production and principle of understanding and explaining the political and law system and ethical norms based on economic relations and realizing unification of compliance with laws and goals of social and economic development through social practices, etc. These principles provide scientific world outlook and methodology for us to scientifically understand the complicated economic phenomena.

(2) Correct position and values. Why are the problems about human beings the fundamental matters of principle in research on philosophy and social sciences? Marxist political economics are the political economics of labor and represents interests of broad masses of laboring people. By integrating laws of economic development and goals of people's practices, it scientifically proves the historical inevitability of socialism replacing capitalism and, on such a basis, proposes the social ideal of the elimination of exploitation and

polarization, realization of free and all-around development of people and achievement of prosperity for all social members. In contemporary China, to adhere to the position and values of Marxism, we shall insist on people orientation, place the fundamental interests of the overwhelming majority of people as the starting point and finishing point for all considerations, lead all people to steadily advance to common prosperity and insist on the social ideal of Marxism and integrate promotion of economic and social development and the all-around development of people, thus to promote and realize the goal of all-around development of people.

(3) General laws for social production. Marxist political economics unveil general laws for social production and propose many important theories, such as the theory of conservation of labor time as the primary economic law of people; theory of distribution of social labor in proportion; theory of primacy of production and relations among production, distribution, exchange and consumption; theory of approaches and methods to improve productivity of labor; theory of general content and basic elements of labor course; theory of development laws of division and coordination; and theory of division of two major categories of social reproduction and their relations, etc. These theories are of significant value in understanding laws and phenomena of economic development. For example, as for how to understand the essence of development, Marx once proposed the penetrating insight that the social development is fundamentally the development of productivity, while the development of productivity equals to the conservation of labor time, equals to the development of personal talents, equals to science increasingly becoming the major driving force for production, equals to compromise between people and nature, equals to added free time and equals to free and all-around development of individuals. This conclusion perfectly integrates the development of productivity, society and people, which greatly inspires us on promoting scientific development.

(4) General laws for commodity production and market economy. Some people believe that as Marx's *Capital* advocates planned economy, it thus has no guiding significance for the socialist market economy. This is completely a misunderstanding. As a matter of fact, the object of studying *Capital* is exactly to study the capitalist market economy instead of the planned economy. Marxist political economics profoundly research on the commodity economy and market economy and analyze the essence and laws of economic phenomena including value, currency, price, supply and demand, competition, cost, profit, credit, information and rent, etc., particularly the essence and operating laws of capital. Ignoring the capitalist production relations, these laws are also applicable for socialist market economy. A great progress and contribution of Marxist political economics in the contemporary age lies in that it proposes the theory of the socialist market economy and successfully establishes the socialist market economy system in practices. By abandoning the capitalist market economy, the socialist market economy reflects the principle of universality of the market economy and the basic features of the socialist system,

gives full play to advantages of the socialist system and market economy and, therefore, goes beyond the current dogma in capitalist market economy based on the private ownership in terms of both theories and practices.

(5) Essence and operating laws of capitalist economy. Marxist political economics clarify the historical trend of generation, development and destruction of capitalism and propose many important theories of capitalist economy, such as the theories of surplus production, residual value distribution, capital accumulation, circulation of capital, reproduction of the social capital and capitalist economic crisis. As proved by the history and realities of capitalist economic development again and again, the basic Marxist principles of capitalist economy would never go obsolete as long as the capitalist system and the relations of capital and labor exist. Studies on theories of capitalist economy of Marxist political economics play an essential role in helping us scientifically understand the essence, characteristics and development trend of contemporary capitalist economy; master the trend of world development; plan the domestic and foreign overall situation as a whole; promote opening up in a healthier and more effective way; and enhance socialist modernization construction in China under globalization.

(6) Economic characteristics of communism and socialism. Through profound analysis of conflicts, operating laws and development trends of capitalist mode of production, Marx and Engels unveiled basic characteristics of the communist and socialist economic relations in the future, including the important ideas on realizing free and all-around development of people, public ownership of means of production replacing the private ownership, distribution according to one's needs and according to one's labor, realization of common prosperity of all social members, proportional development of social production as planned and the elimination of three major differences, respectively, between urban and rural area, workers and peasants and mental labor and physical labor. They also clarified the general goal and essence of socialism and pointed out the basic trend of historical development of society, which became the important guidance for socialist revolution and socialist construction.

Therefore, without Marxism as a guidance and Marxist political economics, we could never scientifically understand laws of current capitalist economy and socialist economy, acquire victory in socialist economic construction with Chinese characteristics, or establish the scientific socialist political economics with Chinese characteristics.

III.   Promote development and innovation of Marxist economics

Marxism is a science subject to constant development. It is necessary to adhere to Marxism's essence of keeping us with the times to develop the economics of China and constantly promote development and innovation of Marxist economics based on practices of Reform and Opening Up.

First, to hold a scientific attitude toward Marxist economics, particularly the theories of authors of Marxist classics on the socialist economy in the future, the followings shall be attached importance to. (1) The basic ideas of Marxism must be adhered to, such as replacing the private ownership with public ownership of the means of production and realizing common prosperity of society. By deviating from these theories, it means to renounce basic principles of scientific socialism. (2) Some ideas in works of authors of Marxist classics have been ignored or simplified due to various subjective and objective causes, such as "the free and all-around development of human beings" and "rebuilding individual ownership", which shall be radically reformed from the bottom. (3) Some theories from authors of Marxist classics may be inconsistent with current practical conditions and shall be corrected based on the development of practices. For example, Marx and Engels once made a statement on the non-commodity-money relationship in socialism. (4) Due to restricted historical conditions, authors of Marxist classics did not make profound discussion and research on many new conditions and issues. It is necessary to conduct in-depth research and give a scientific explanation and description according to the standpoint, view and methods of Marxism, such as the issues related to the information-oriented economy and socialist market economy.

Second, theories must be combined with practices in socialist economic construction with Chinese characteristics, so as to constantly accelerate the localization of Marxist economics in China. Major approaches to localize Marxist economics in China include the follows:

The first is to apply basic principles of scientific socialism in a correct way. For example, basic principles of scientific socialism have been enriched by exploring the specific mechanism, scope of application and implementation procedure of public ownership and distribution according to work from practices of China and establishing the modern enterprise system of state-owned enterprises and rural land contract system based on adherence to public ownership of the means of production and distribution according to work.

The second is to develop basic principles of scientific socialism, such as proposing new ideas in a creative way including the basic economic system of the primary stage of socialism, building a well-off society in an all-around way, construction of new socialist countryside and opening up to capitalist countries, which have developed basic principles of scientific socialism.

The third is the innovation of basic principles of scientific socialism. For example, it was a basic principle of scientific socialism where no commodity-money exists in future society, and the planned economy should be applied. We have corrected the principle based on practices and proposed the theory of socialist market economy, making up significant innovation of Marxism and scientific socialism theories.

Third, combine theories with the present era to promote modernization of Marxist economics and particularly promote development and innovation of basic theories of Marxist economics based on practices and experiences in China. The criteria on the judgment of the superiority of the socialist system can be taken as an instance. As it is a basic principle of Marxist economics that productive forces determine the relations of productivity, we have proposed the important idea where productive forces shall be applied as the fundamental standard for achievements of work and revolution since Reform and Opening Up based on the principle. This is correct beyond any doubt. However, it leads to a question – i.e., how to regard the relationship between the development of productive forces and improvement of socialist system – which is the question of the relation between objective facts and value judgment, and normative economics and positive economics.

The issue is derived from an inherent sharp contradiction always existing in theories of scientific socialism. According to historical materialism, social beings determine social consciousness, and productive forces determine the relations of production, so the development of productive forces undoubtedly constitutes the basic drive for social progress and fundamental criterion for judgment on the progress of institutional transformation. However, from the other perspective, socialism is a movement pushed forward by constant practices and a distant ideal that can only be realized through tenacious pursuit and efforts; so, if we have no great value pursuit or target guidance, or we have no passion or expectation about the socialist movement, what is the significance of socialist movements? This contradiction has been bothering socialists ever since the birth of scientific socialism. Many wrong understandings in the history of socialist movements result from the wrong understanding or treatment of the contradiction.

The contradiction between the criterion of productive forces and criterion of value has been increasingly highlighted during current economic reform and development in China. On the one hand, the economic aggregate has shown constant and rapid development for over three decades at a rate of approximately 10%, and, on the other hand, polarization between the rich and poor, widespread corruption, overflow of moral egoism and capitalist factors are exerting growing influence. Therefore, the issue of the consistency between the criterion of productive forces and the institutional or value criterion is confronting us, and we have to think deeply about a series of major theoretical issues, including what is development of productive forces, how to measure development of productive forces, what is the basis and system for the productive forces determining the relations of productivity and the attribute and results of the counter-action of the relations of production against the productive forces and so on. Most importantly, is the productive forces the only criterion of judgment of the advancement of a kind of social economic system and what is the relation between the criterion of productive forces and the institutional or value criterion? No profound research on these basic theoretical issues and no scientific understanding acquired will cause chaos in guiding ideas and may even lead to major directional deviation. In recent years, the theoretical circle in China has made profound discussion on these issues and achieved favorable results. For example, some scholars have proposed that two criteria shall be held to for judgment on socialist economic system – i.e., integration of the criterion of productive forces and value criterion. In practical life, we have gone through four different situations. First, we combined the two criteria, when the socialist economy and society were exposed to successful development. Second, we attached importance to the development of productive forces superficially but carried out the Great Leap Forward that violates laws in development of productive forces, and we emphasized values of socialism and communism superficially but violated development laws of the relations of production and advocated the "communism wind", leading to loss of productive forces and disasters to people. Third, we ignored development of productive forces and put undue emphasis on the socialist road, "cutting the tail of capitalism", and it resulted in socialism of mass poverty, which deviated from the criterion of productive forces and at the same time distorted the value criterion. Fourth, we focused and emphasized on the criterion of productive forces but ignored the socialist value criterion, and, as a result, the polarization between the rich and poor emerged, which deviated from the requirement on eliminating polarization and achieving common prosperity and even shocked and damaged socialist economic system.[5] In view of historical experiences, we shall integrate the two issues under socialist system together. Deng Xiaoping had put forward the essence of socialism, which integrated the two criteria. Within the essence of socialism proposed by him, liberation and development of the productive forces constitute the criterion on productive forces, and the elimination of exploitation and polarization, and the ultimate achievement of prosperity for all, make up the criterion on values. It is a value criterion that socialism aims at the elimination of exploitation and polarization, and the ultimate achievement of prosperity for all. Some scholars do not agree with the earlier opinion and adhere to the only criterion on productive forces. Regardless of everyone's different opinions, it is affirmed that discussion and research on this issue are necessary. We need to deepen our understanding along with the development of theories and practices.

IV.   Draw lessons from western economics correctly

Marxist economics was generated and developed through constant dialogue and confrontation with western bourgeois economics. As Lenin pointed out,

> Marxism shares no similarity with 'sectarianism'. It is absolutely not a kind of doctrine standing still and refusing to make progress which was generated as deviated from the development path of world civilization. On the contrary, all gifts of Marx lie where he had replied to the problems proposed by advanced thinking of people. His theories directly carried over ideas of extremely great representatives of philosophy, political economics and socialism.[6]

It is necessary to correctly draw lessons from western economic theories and well handle the relationship between Marxist economics and western economics, so as to push forward the development of economic theories and practices in China.

First, we shall admit that western economics includes something rational and useful which deserve our careful learning and can be mainly manifested by the three aspects that follow:

(1) Various schools of western economics have reflected certain laws of the market economy and distribution of resources to a certain degree, such as theories of price movement, growth and fluctuations, money and finance, international trade, changes in interest rate and the exchange rate, industrial

organization and enterprises and institutional changes. Researches on specific economic phenomena and laws of economic operations have continued for hundreds of years in theories of western economics, with an increasingly larger scope and increasingly detailed content of research. With new theories and new ideas emerging in an endless stream, it improves people's understanding about laws of economic life and operation.

(2) Analysis methods in western economics play a positive role in the development of economic science, such as marginal analysis, statistics and measurement, input-output, experiment and currently popular game theory. Particularly, the wide application of mathematical method makes a significant feature of modern western economics. The wide application of mathematical method could clearly and accurately express the assumption, deduction and conclusion of theories, so its correct application exerts the beneficial effect on the development of economic theories.

(3) Theories of different schools of western economics reflect thoughts on the essence of economic life and the movement laws of different people in different ages. Even though some of them have been proved to be incorrect, they are valuable for us as we can summarize experiences and lessons and understand the development of economic thoughts. For example, the argument on free trade theory and protective trade theory in the UK in the 19th century reflected the different interests of industrial capitalists and landlord class at that time, and the argument between German historical school and UK classical school suggested different requirements of relatively backward German capitalism and advanced UK capitalism.

Due to the rationality and usefulness of western economics, we shall not completely deny and reject it, but shall scientifically learn from and use it for reference. However, we also shall not mechanically copy or blindly worship western economics or even regard it as the only scientific theory. Instead, we shall use it in a critical way, apply it in certain conditions, absorb its rational part and abandon the factor of ideology in it for following causes.

First, western economics has dual characters, namely the rational and useful part as well as the factor of ideology that cannot be denied. This has been evidently manifested in the basic theories of western economics. For example, the important theories in western economics such as the "hypothesis of economic man", subjective value theory, factor value theory, human capital theory, perfect competition theory and freedom first, directly defending the capitalist system. Though they cannot be verified by facts or experiences and show serious defects in logic, they meet the interests and requirements of relevant economic parties and are therefore popular in capitalist countries. As admitted by some modern western economists, western economics contains the prejudice of ideology. As pointed out by Robert M. Solow, the winner of Noble Prize for Economics and American economics,

> Same with other people, social scientists have their own value judgment on class interests, preference in ideology and other kinds of staff. However,

different with researches on mechanics of materials or chemical molecular structure, studies on social sciences are related to the above (class) interests, ideology and value judgment. No matter what the social scientist is hoping for and whether he has realized the problem and even though he tried to avoid the influence, his selection about the research subject, the problem he proposes and fails to propose, his analysis framework and language he uses possibly reflect his (class) interests, ideology and value judgment to certain degree.[7]

Second, western economics consist of various schools with different ideas, and no so-called scientific theory has been commonly accepted by all ages and all people. For example, also as the mainstream economist, Joseph Stiglitz strongly criticizes neoclassical economics. He believes that neoclassical economics has many fundamental defects, such as not recognizing the significance of incentive problem, overrating the role of price, not understanding difficulties in capital allocation, lacking a correct understanding of the role and function of decentralization and competition and ignoring the role of technical innovation in economics.[8] Within the same neoliberalism economics, different schools showed up including the Neo-Austrian school represented by Ludwig Von Mises and Friedrich Von Hayek, the London school represented by Edwin Cannan and Lionel C. Robbins, Chicago school represented by Milton Friedman and the neo-institutionalism represented by R. H. Coase and Douglass C. North and so on. Despite the academic community generated based on the promotion of private ownership and free market economy, they criticize and oppose each other on some specific issue. For example, neo-institutionalism scientists believe that the neoclassical economics is the theory about market operation instead of the theory of market generation and it is imperfect since it abandons time and makes institutions abstract. Austrian school thinks that the market mechanism is not a mechanism for resources allocation but a mechanism for knowledge and information exchange, and as the knowledge and information are subjective and mastered by individuals in a decentralized way, so the so-called general equilibrium does not exist. This argument between different schools of western economics is academically normal, but it also demonstrates that there is no so-called universal scientific truth.

Third, some theories of western economics that seem correct at certain times are established upon certain assumptions, historical experiences, value orientation, cultural background and logistics structure. Therefore, we cannot mechanically copy these theories but shall combine practices in China. Gunnar Myrdal, the famous Swedish economist, once pointed out,

These (western) economic terms were abstracted from the living method, living standard, altitude, system and culture of the western world, so they may be meaningful to analyze the western world and reach the correct conclusion, but absolutely will not get the correct conclusion in less developed countries.[9]

For example, the market economy needs some general factors or fundamental framework, such as independent enterprises, adequate competition and free price. By further abstracting these factors, the ideal theory of perfect competition market is formed. However, in practical economic life, it takes conditions and time to form these factors or framework, which is difficult to complete. The so-called ideal market and perfect competition market can only be considered as a hypothesis in theory instead of the basis for making decisions in practices. For another instance, the free trade theory is a basic principle of mainstream economics. However, a country would only apply the policy of free trade when it owns competitive edges in the international market in practices but intends to adopt the protective tariff system during primitive accumulation of capital and establishment of its own industrial system. Actually, the UK, Germany, France and the United States had all once applied the protective tariff system in history without any exception.

The complexity of the problem lies in that the useful part and the part of ideology in western economics are often mixed together and are not separated. Therefore, without scientific discriminating ability or careful examination, we may easily apply the harmful part in western economics as the useful part but ignore the truly rational and useful part. Here two instances are given.

The first is how to understand the relation between the government and the market. Many ideas on this question are widely spread, such as the "big market and small government", "and small government and big society"; it will be better if the government manages fewer, which only serves the market and enterprises and only provides public products without bearing any more functions, and, in the market economy, government is only the referee and server instead of the player, so it shall not bear more functions than maintaining the market order and providing public services. These ideas seem to be discussing on economic systems and reflecting laws of resources allocation, but they actually reflect the ideology of neoliberalism. This is because in the capitalist system, the market plays the role of capital, particularly the role of monopoly capital. As pointed out by Karl Marx long time ago, the so-called free trade is actually the freedom of capital, which "eliminates all obstacles that inhibit the movement of capitals".[10] Any conscious social supervision and adjustment during the course of social production are branded the "originality" that infringes capitalists' property right, freedom and self-determination. Chomsky, the famous American modern scholar, had once pungently pointed out that the theories and policies of neoliberalism "represent the direct interests of extremely rich investors and no more than 1,000 huge companies", which are merely the modern name for the few rich people to restrict common people's rights.[11] Paul R. Krugman concludes the essence of neoliberalism movement as "returning to the past and setting back economic policies that inhibit inequality" and bringing America back to the age when the small number of rich people ruled before the Great Depression.[12]

The second is how to understand economic efficiency. In modern western economics, efficiency is publicly known as a purely objective concept that has nothing to do with value judgment. It seems unquestionable to judge people's economic activities with efficiency. However, it is not the case. In fact, people's moral judgment and efficiency judgment affect each other in a complicated and undefined way. In terms of efficiency judgment, the concept of efficiency itself is based on certain controversial assumptions, and, when a specific social arrangement satisfies a criterion of efficiency, the judgment on its significance and importance is directly related to people's value judgment. This is because the efficiency is a result based on comparison or measurement of cost and revenue, or input and output, but different people in different background of history, culture and social system hold different understanding about what is the cost and what is the revenue. The efficiency of primitive men is different from the efficiency of slave owners, the efficiency of feudal lords is different from the efficiency of capitalists, the macro-efficiency of a country is different from the micro-efficiency of an enterprise, the short-term efficiency is different from the long-term efficiency and the efficiency of technology is different from the efficiency of currency. For example, the returns acquired by chemical plants that produce pollution may result in the cost of the polluted enterprises; the returns of people of the current age increased by the exhaustion of global resources may bring about the huge loss of the later generation; the salary is the workers' return but the cost of capitalists, and the profit is the capitalists' return but the payment of laborers, and though the economic subsidies for certain areas, enterprises and individuals (such as subsidies to poor areas, basic industries and the unemployed) do not meet requirements on short-term efficiency of the market, they facilitate the improvement of macro and dynamic efficiency and so on.

In recent years, a new kind of dogmatism became popular in Chinese economic circle. It believes that the western mainstream economics is the only kind of economics in this world, which is scientific and universal without any restriction on nation or boundary, and we shall believe and learn from it without any question, as it is the direction of the development of Chinese economics and shall completely fulfill and practice it, as it is the direction of Chinese economic reform. This is a new kind of obscurantism. We can never truly establish the self-consciousness and confidence if we do not get rid of the dogmatism and obscurantism. After the financial crisis in 2008, Paul R. Krugman once stated, "To put it nicely, the research achievements of macro-economics in past three decades are useless, and, to put it bluntly, they are even harmful".[13] Joseph Stiglitz was more straightforward:

> The fundamentalism of neoliberal market is the political dogmas always serving for certain interests, which has never been supported by theories of economics, now, clearly, and never been supported by historical experiences. It may be the little hope of the dark world economy by drawing lessons from it.

Since mainstream scholars in the west make practical appraisal about their own theories, why do some Chinese economic scholars still be so superstitious about these western theories?

Theories are actually the reflection of real life and summary of practical experiences, and necessarily develop along with the development of the reality and practices. There is no eternal and universal economics without a certain background of history and real life. Same as the development of human civilization, development of economics always result from mutual exchange, collision and integration of ideas and theories proposed by people at different ages and in different countries based on their own practices and experiences, and is never the patent of a certain country or certain individual. In the development course of human history, the Chinese nation has not been and should never be the imitator or follower of theories of other countries, but shall make certain invention, creation and contribution. Any mechanic copy of theories and experiences of other countries will completely fail due to diversified and vigorous practices. It shall be noted that the blind worship and copy of western theories and experiences not only deviate from Chinese practices and fail to solve problems in China but also make us slaves of certain wrong ideas, lead to loss of independence and creativity in theories and ideas, even spread and impose the special experiences, interests and ideology of western countries on China as the "universal value" and endanger the undertakings of socialism with Chinese characteristics. Therefore, we must maintain keen vigilance at times and never let down our guard.

V.   Openness, communication and inclusive tolerance

Same as all other sciences, openness, communication and inclusive tolerance are required for the prosperity and development of economics in China, to find out the guide and common sense in diversity and lead the trend. It is a pity that openness, communication and inclusive tolerance are not the mainstream of economics in China, while it is fashionable to pursue standardization and acting on international convention. In addition to the restrictions on the age, practice and class of economics, other evident mistakes exist in the so-called pursuit of standardization and acting on international convention, not only popular theories in different countries and different ages are different but also in the same country and same age – for example, the current America. Different schools hold to different opinions, with some growing and some declining. If talking about the standardization and acting on international convention, the problems lie in that which "convention" and how to "act". In fact, the standardization advocated by many people right now refers to Americanization, to be more specific, to be more neoclassical. However, the neoclassical economics is definitely not a perfect and universal theory but exists with severe defects, mainly including focus on logic, looking down on history, focus on the form, setting down the content, denying differences of people's behaviors in different social systems and historical conditions, ignorance of the effect of complicated factors such as technology, system, politics and culture on economic life, regarding pursuit of maximum personal interests of so-called economic men as the starting point to think about all problems, considering the market economy of capitalism as the eternal economic form of people and applying the abstract mathematical logic as the main criteria to judge whether the economics is scientific, etc. We can only conditionally absorb and critically learn from the theory, but shall not regard it as the only standard for acting on international convention.

Here, we shall hold a correct attitude toward the so-called mainstream economics. Generally, the so-called mainstream economics is the economic theory widely recognized and agreed by the majority of economists and policy makers. Based on such a standard, it is an undoubted fact that western mainstream economics is exerting increasingly greater influence in China. In addition to the severe disadvantages of the mainstream economics, it is harmful to worship mainstream economics and denounce the non-mainstream economics too much purely from the perspective of the development of thoughts and learning. The mainstream and non-mainstream are relative historical concept and are not fixed. A certain theory of economics may become the mainstream theory or policy as it complies with the interests and values of the ruling class at that time but also may be replaced by other theories as the mainstream theory along with changes to historical conditions. A certain new non-mainstream theory may also become the mainstream theory under proper conditions. For example, in the UK and France, mercantilism was popular in the 16th century, classical economics was popular from the 17th century to the 19th century, the neoclassical economics was popular in late 19th century and early 20th century, and Keynesianism became the mainstream economics after the economic crisis of the capitalist world. Since the 1970s, due to increasing internal economic and social conflicts of capitalism, Keynesianism lost its mainstream status to the monetarism and rational expectations school that advocates free market. The changes to the mainstream and non-mainstream status will never stop in the future. Moreover, mainstream economics may be different in different countries of the same age. For example, in the 19th century, the classical economics represented by Adam Smith and David Ricardo was popular in the UK, while the historical school had been the mainstream theory in Germany at that time. In Japan, due to the special historical environment, Marxist economics has dominated the significant status in education and study of economics since the 20th century.

Moreover, restricted by interests and values of the ruling class, the mainstream economics is not necessarily more scientific and reasonable than the non-mainstream economics. For example, after the 1830s, in order to reconcile the increasingly violent class contradiction, some bourgeois economics represented by James Mill, John McCulloch, Nassau Senior, Henry Carey and Frederic Bastiat abandoned the scientific classical political economics and established the vulgar economics mentioned by Karl Marx. The vulgar economics became the mainstream theory of economics at that time. However, it could not demonstrate that the vulgar economics is more scientific than classical economics. On the contrary, according to Karl Marx, the classical economics attempted to explore the internal relation of the capitalist mode of production and seek for the objective economic laws through economic phenomena, while the latter one was satisfied by describing the external relation of the capitalist mode of production and denied the objective economic laws behind the phenomena by highlighting the appearance of phenomena; the classical economics tried to reveal economic relations and objective laws supporting the opinions and behaviors of relevant parties instead of being restricted by opinions of the relevant parties in production and operation in the capitalist economic relations, while the vulgar economics only summarized the opinions of the relevant parties in capitalist production and operation as a system and theory and announced it as the eternal truth; the classical economics held a critical altitude, presented the faithfulness of science and dared to say things that the progressive and revolutionary bourgeoisie wanted to say, while the vulgar economics was economics for defense and satisfied and adapted the science to the private interests of bourgeoisie instead of pursuing the scientific truth with no fear. The scientificalness of modern mainstream neoclassical economics is also questionable, not only the non-mainstream economics including numerous schools such as the institutional economics, neo-political economics, evolution economics and radical economics have profoundly criticized this theory from many perspectives but also mainstream economists such as Joseph Stiglitz believe that the new-classical economics based on the "Invisible Hand" of Adam Smith plays a little role in the transition economy and institutional selection and even shows fundamental restrictions in explaining the advanced market economy. For our Chinese economists, it is irrational for us to worship western mainstream economics blindly regardless of the fundamental tasks of construction and development of economics in China, or even apply it as the only truth and impose on Chinese practices.

To develop economics in China and build the economics system and academic discourse system of China, it is required to overcome the one-sided dogmatism on standardization and internationalization and lead the path of openness, communication, inclusive tolerance and extensive learning.

- Learn from all nations and all countries, not only studying from experiences and theories of economic development in developed countries but also learning those experiences and theories from extensive developing countries.
- Learn from history and traditions. Studies on both domestic and foreign history, on economic development and the domestic and foreign history, on the development of economic theories and thoughts inherit the ideological heritage created by ancestors and respect the cultural traditions formed in history.
- Learn from all sciences. Learn from all achievements of natural sciences as well as achievements of philosophy, politics, history, sociology, literature and fine art and other humanities and social sciences.
- Learn from all schools, including mainstream economics such as neoclassical economics and New Keynesian Economics and non-mainstream economics such as Keynesian economics, institutional economics, evolution economics and radical economics.
- Learn from practices and the masses. A study from new experiences created by people in socialist construction, routes, principles and policies of the Party and government to guide and promote the development of practices as well as the investigation reports and policy consulting by relevant decision-making authorities, research institutions, experts and scholars.

VI.   Master the general and special dialectics

One important characteristic of the methodology of western mainstream economics is worshiping universality and generality, rejecting particularity and individuality, reflecting on questions through hypothesis of axiom, deduction and model and applying the abstract theories in textbooks to shape the diversified reality, while these so-called general principles are based on particular theories, especially the neoclassical economics. As controlled by this kind of logic of thinking, the standard explanation of Chinese experiences that follows is formed. Chinese experiences belong to "economics of transition" – i.e., the transition to the perfect capitalist market, without any universal meaning of economics. As development = marketization = liberalization, it will finally lead to urbanization and globalization. The service industry will force out agriculture and manufacturing. The border between and the role of countries will disappear, while only individuals and enterprises (consumers, producers and investors) last forever. The reason for the capitalism finally conquering socialism is the selfishness of human nature. The experiment of socialist industrialization in the former Soviet Union and the first three decades of China is a historical mistake, etc.[14] Any success of the Chinese economy shall be attributed to the effective application of general principles of the mainstream economics, such as the development of private economy, market adjustment and opening up, while the problems of the Chinese economy emerge because China deviated from these general principles, such as maintaining the state-owned economy, government interference and independence of the Chinese economy would be exposed to collapse if these problems cannot be solved. In conclusion, any behavior that does not comply with the standard model of the mainstream economics is considered as the deviation from or distortion of general rules. Obviously, the logic is completely wrong and extremely harmful and shows evident metaphysics.

We know that the generality is based on the personality, while the universality is contained in the particularity, which is applicable to all theories. Modern western economics enjoys certain generality or universality as it reflects the laws of market economy operation to a certain degree; at the same time, it also shows personality or particularity. Various schools of western economics hold various opinions, and only a few are recognized as the general theories. Even some theories widely considered correct by people are established based on the condition of certain space and time. Different social and economic systems present differences in time and space, which is known as "historical and geographical issue".[15] Generally speaking, the modern western economics was generated based on the market economy and was not applicable to non-market economic systems, such as the primitive society, slave society, feudal society and planning economy. Even for the market economy, its applicability is still questioned due to differences between the socialist market economy and capitalist market economy. The capitalist market economy is currently the most advanced market economy, so people may regard it as the model and consider particular laws of the capitalist market economy as the general laws or "international conventions". However, it is not the case. The capitalist market economy is still the integration of the generality and particularity and subject to the dialectics of generality and particularity. As is known to all, the labor becoming the commodity, the capital hiring the labor, production of the surplus value, generation of average profits, emergence of monopoly capital and worldwide economic crisis due to common overproduction are not the inborn phenomena of the market economy, but the product of transition from the small commodity production and capitalist commodity production. In the socialist market economy based on public ownership, though the aforementioned phenomena may not completely disappear, they would be well controlled and regulated and subject to major changes, and, meanwhile, some new economic laws and characteristics may also emerge.

We shall pay special attention to the fact that the theory of socialist economy with Chinese characteristics summarized from practices and experiences of China is not the particular thing of China and cannot be simply considered a case or exception. It is no doubt that the experiences of economic reform and development in China are the product of the particular national conditions of China. The special economic structure, political structure, historical and cultural traditions, special routes, principles and policies and even special style of the leadership constitute the Chinese characteristics. Therefore, Chinese experiences are not applicable to all countries. However, we shall not separate Chinese characteristics with generality or universality or even set them against each other, which does not comply with dialectics. The generality is based on the personality. Practically, all important issues encountered in economic reform and development in China are also the issues for all countries especially developing countries, such as industrialization, information, urbanization, macro-economic stability, development of the market system, innovation of the enterprise control structure, relation between the central and local government, openness to the outside, construction of democratic politics and inheritance and development of traditional culture. Generation, development and effective solution of these issues absolutely adhere to general laws. Therefore, Chinese experiences necessarily contain some universal and general things. Take one case for example. As is known to all, regardless of socialist countries or capitalist countries, people's understanding of the market economy had been one-sided for a very long period and all believed that market economy was only applicable to capitalism and only capitalism could adopt the market economy and socialism could not. This kind of understanding set up a huge obstacle to people's horizon. The Communist Party of China broke off this traditional idea with huge theoretical and historical courage, proposed the theory of socialist market economy, established the socialist market economic system and realized the integration of socialism and market economy for the first time in the human history. It revealed the general principles of the market economy, meanwhile reflected the basic characteristics of the socialist system, realized the combination of efficiency and equality, plan and market, independence and openness and the dominant role of public ownership and co-development of various types of ownerships, and gave the full play to the advantages of both socialist system and market economy. The theory of socialist market economy not only makes great contributions to the theory of Marxism and scientific socialism but also provides enlightenments and experiences for extensive developing countries of the current world, which are trying to get rid of poverty and realize national development. Therefore, it is particular and meanwhile general. As pointed out by Xi Jinping, the more national it is, the more international it is. By solving the national issues, we are more capable of solving international issues; ad by summarizing Chinese practices, we are more capable of providing thoughts and methods for solving the international issues. This is the law of development from particularity to universality.[16] Many similar cases can be put forward here. People generally believe that practices of economic reform and development in China have broadened the vision of study on economics, diversify people's thoughts on economics study, deepen people's understanding about the market economy and institutional transition and propose challenges too many general theories of western mainstream economics. One important task of contemporary Chinese economics lies in extracting ideas and innovating theories based on Chinese experiences, upgrading the particularity to the universality and thus promoting the development of theories of economics.

VII. Integration of logic and history

One inevitable result of worshiping generality and universality and rejecting particularity and personality is worshiping logic deduction and rejecting historical analysis. It has been a significant tradition of bourgeois economics to consider the capitalist market economy as certain transcendental trans-historical phenomenon since the age of Adam Smith and David Ricardo. From this perspective, the modern western economics is going even further. According to this idea, the market system formed in the capitalist society is not the product of historical development but the starting point of historical development, is not the result of production development but the prerequisite of production development, is not generated based on objective historical conditions but created by human nature. Meanwhile, the western mainstream economics based on understandings, ideas and expressions of the capitalist parties is considered as the eternal truth. For example, the hypothesis of economic man is deemed as an axiom with no need to prove it; private ownership is considered the manifestation of human nature of selfishness; the free contract is considered men's natural rights; the cost-return analysis is regarded as the starting point of all people's behaviors, and the theory of comparative advantages is taken as the trans-historical scientific principle like the theorem in physics. As influenced by these ideas, the education and research on history of economic thinking and economic history have been severely damaged. The history and ancestors have been forgotten, traditions have been cast away, it has been mechanically copied in many places, and history nihilism is widely spread. Obviously, if guiding reform with these ideas, it will definitely lead to subversive error and the mistake of changing the whole system.

Political economics is essentially a historical science. As pointed out by Engels,

> Conditions for production and exchange of people are different in differ-
> ent countries; and though in the same country, they vary in different ages.
> Therefore, political economics is not the same for all countries and all ages.
> If anyone views political economics of Tierra del Fuego and political eco-
> nomics of modern UK with the same law, he could hardly unveil anything
> other than the platitude. In this way, political economics is essentially a his-
> torical science. It firstly involves historical information subject to constant
> change, studies on special laws of production and exchange in each indi-
> vidual development phase and upon completion of these studies, confirms
> on the small number of completely universal laws applicable to general
> production and exchange.[17]

Joseph Schumpeter once said, "Anyone who does not know historical facts or have
any historical sense or so-called historical experiences can never understand the
economic phenomena of any age (including the present)".[18] When summarizing
Chinese experiences in reform and developing economics theories in China, it
is necessary to carefully study on Chinese history and absorb nutrients from the
history. As pointed out by Xi Jinping,

> The 5000-year history of civilization of the Chinese nation, the 170-year his-
> tory of the struggle of Chinese people in modern times, the 90-year history
> of the Communist Party of China, the 60-year history of development of the
> People's Republic of China and the 30-year history of exploration in reform
> come down in one continuous line and cannot be separated from each other.
> It is difficult to correctly understand China if separating it from Chinese his-
> tory, Chinese culture, Chinese people's spiritual world and profound reform
> in contemporary China.[19]

Chinese economics grows up from the rich soil of Chinese economic history and
history of economic thinking. Only by deeply rooting in the rich soil of history,
Chinese economics could make development vigorously and endlessly

As is known to all, the road of socialism with Chinese characteristics formed
in the three decades after Reform and Opening Up has been established based
on the history of socialist construction in the three decades before Reform and
Opening Up. The unique theoretical results and great achievements made during
the socialist construction by the Party provided precious experiences, theoretical
preparation and material basis for the creation of socialism with Chinese characteristics in the new historical period. Without seeing the close link between
the first three decades and the latter three decades, it is impossible to understand the internal logic of economic reform in China. When analyzing the success
of the gradual reform in China, domestic and foreign scholars both discover
the fact that the success of gradual reform in China shows a close relation with

some favorable initial conditions equipped at the beginning of the Reform. The *Role of Reform and Planning in the 1990s*, the investigation report on Chinese economy by the World Bank, once concluded the favorable initial conditions for Chinese reform as the lagging return of materials investment before the Reform. For example, infrastructure for agriculture including materials, sales and labors has been established during the period of People's Commune, but the incentive factor was lacked in agriculture. Once the personal incentive measure was introduced and the role of the government was reformed, the rapid development of output would be foreseen. For another example, the industrialization has been significantly improved after 1949, particularly the heavy industry and big and medium-sized state-owned enterprises. On the one hand, it meant that China had already the basis for construction of industry of a large scale, and, on the other hand, after the investment was lowered to people, many investment opportunities in the light industry could be found.[20] There are a great number of instances like this.

To understand the economic reform in contemporary China, it is necessary to link to the socialist revolution and construction for decades as well as the development history of the Chinese nation for thousands of years. Being a country with long history, ancient civilization, deep-rooted traditions and broad and profound culture, it renders rich and profound historical heritage for social transition. Like an invisible hand, history is leading the direction of the Reform of the age. People have diversified opinions on the relationship between Chinese traditional culture and market economy and modernization. However, people can hardly deny the inherent relation between the two. For example, Chinese traditional culture is established on the core of familism, while the land management system based on family contract adopted since the Reform is actually a new form of the ancient familism. Moreover, in a very long period, the social security in China, particularly in rural area, was provided based on the traditional extended family, which significantly saved the cost of social security of the government and enterprise, increased the household saving rate and was very beneficial to economic growth.

Theories reflect practices. Along with the vigorous development of undertakings of socialism with Chinese characteristics and the great rejuvenation of the Chinese nation, theories necessarily usher in prosperous development. It is an indispensable part of the prosperity of theories in China to promote theoretical confidence about Chinese economics and develop the economics theories and academic discourse system of Chinese characteristics and the features of the age that are applicable to Chinese history, culture, system and practices. The new theories and discourse system still demand further exploration and innovation, but the direction shall be clear as follows: adhere to the guidance by Marxism, learn from excellent achievements of foreign countries, base in China, face the world, root in the history, serve the reality, keep openness, communication and inclusive tolerance and provide theoretical support to the construction of the modern socialist power and the great rejuvenation of the Chinese nation.

Notes

1 Mao Zedong, *Speech at the Chinese Communist Party's National Conference on Propaganda Work*, March 12, 1957, Vol. 7 of *Collections of Mao Zedong*, People's Publishing House, Edition 1999, Page 281.
2 Xi Jinping, "Speech at the 23rd Collective Learning of the Political Bureau of the CPC Central Committee", *People's Daily*, November 25, 2015.
3 Deng Xiaoping, *Speech at the Third Plenary Session of Central Advisory Commission of the CPC*, October 22, 1984, Vol. 3 of *Selected Works of Deng Xiaoping*, People's Publishing House, Edition 1994, Page 83.
4 Karl Marx, *Capital*, Vol. 1, People's Publishing House, Edition 2004, Page 92.
5 Wei Xinghua, "On Integration of Criterion of Socialist Productive Forces and Values", *Economics Information*, 2010, 10th Issue, Page 16–19.
6 Vladimir Lenin, *Three Sources and Three Components of Marxism*, March 1913, Vol. 2 of *Selected Works of Lenin*, People's Publishing House, Edition 2012, Page 309.
7 Quoted from Wu Yifeng, *Marxist Economics and Western Economics*, Economic Science Press, Edition 2002, Page 237–238.
8 Joseph E. Stigliz, *Whither Socialism*, The MIT Press, 1994.
9 [Sweden] Gunnar Myrdal, *Asian Drama, Study on Poverty in South Asian Countries*, translated by Fang Fuqian, Capital University of Economics and Business Press, Edition 2001, Page 9.
10 Karl Marx, *Speech on Free Trade*, January 9, 1848, Vol. 1 of *Selected Works of Marx and Engels*, People's Publishing House, Edition 2012, Page 373.
11 [US] Noam Chomsky, *Neoliberalism and Global Order*, translated by Xu Haiming and Ji Haihong, Jiangsu People's Publishing House, Chinese translation edition, 2000, Page 1 and 6.
12 [US] Paul R. Krugman, *What Happened to America?*, translated by Liu Bo, CITIC Press, Edition 2008, Page 7.
13 Zhao Zhun, "Argument on 'Efficient-market Hypothesis' After Crisis – How Economists Examine and Safeguard the Interior Stability of the Financial Market", *Review on Political Economics*, Vol. 1, 2010, 2nd Issue, Page 138–153.
14 Chen Ping, "Dispute on China's Path and Confusion in Neoclassical Economics", *Political Economic Review*, Vol. 1, 2012, 2nd Issue, Page 39–75.
15 Geoffrey M. Hodgson, *How Does Economics Forget About History: Historical Issues in Social Sciences*, China Renmin University Press, Edition 2008, Page 25.
16 Xi Jinping, "Speech at Symposium on Philosophy and Social Work", *People's Daily*, May 18, 2016.
17 *Selected Works of Marx and Engels*, Vol. 3, People's Publishing House, Edition 2012, Page 525–526.
18 Joseph Schumpeter, *History of Economic Analysis*, Vol. 1, Commercial Press, 1996, Page 29.
19 "Speech of Xi Jinping at College of Europe in Bruges", *Xinhua Net*, April 1, 2014, http://news.xinhuanet.com/politics/2014-04/01/c_1110054309.htm
20 Series of Investigation on Chinese Economy by the World Bank, *Role of Reform and Planning in the 1990s*, China Financial and Economic Publishing House, Edition 1993, Page 4.

2 Political-economics analysis of Chinese economic model

What is the Chinese model? Is there a Chinese model? What is the significance of the Chinese model? This is the most eye-catching topic of the current world. This topic covers abundant content, consisting of economic, political, cultural and social aspects, etc. This article aims to analyze the characteristics and significance of the Chinese economic model from the perspective of political economics. The first section summarizes the evolution and development of recognition of the Chinese economic model; the second section clarifies the major characteristics of the Chinese economic model; the third section analyzes the conflicts and choices encountered by the Chinese economic model, and the fourth section discusses the significance of the Chinese economic model, including the universality and particularity.

I. Evolution and development of recognition of the Chinese economic model

The recognition of and research on the Chinese economic model has been constantly developing along with practices of Chinese socialist construction. As early as the late 1950s – i.e., right after the foundation of the socialist system – the leadership of the first generation represented by Mao Zedong had proposed the guideline to realize the second combination of Marxism and Chines practices and to lead the unique road of China and carry out the initial exploration on the road of socialist construction in China. In the academic circle, a great number of scholars represented by Sun Yefang also conducted in-depth thinking about some major issues in socialist economic construction in China and acquired certain theoretical achievements. In terms of the guiding ideology and course of practices, the development direction of the economic model in China is formed under the theoretical guidance of localized Marxism beyond any doubt. From the academic perspective, different schools and ideas exist on the understanding of the economic model in China, while they have generally experienced the three major development stages as follows since Reform and Opening Up.

(1) Model of comparative economics: discussion on the goal and model of economic system reform in the 1980s

At the early stage of economic reform, on the one hand, practices of economic system reform were proposing increasingly strong demands on theoretical reform, and, on the other hand, the conventional western economics and traditional social-ist economic theories lacked systematic theories of evolution of the market eco-nomic system. Under such circumstances, the theories comparative economics played an important part as the major theoretical support to the exploration of the economic model. Regarding theories, the Chinese academic circle had once attached great importance to theories of the socialist economic system from for-eign scholars from the Soviet Union and Eastern Europe, etc., such as the model of "planned simulation market" from Oskar Lange, the model of "planned economy containing the market system" from Virlyn W. Bruse, the model of "free mar-ket subject to adjustment by macro income distribution plan" from Ota Sik, the model of "market coordination under macro-control" from Janos Kornai and the model of "feasible socialism" from Alec Nove. In terms of practices, people had paid much attention to autonomous socialism in Yugoslavia, the new economic mechanism in Hungary, the New Thinking of Gorbachev and the models of East Asia, Northern Europe and Britain and America. Based on the comparative study, domestic scholars conducted the in-depth discussion on the goal and model of the economic system reform in China and attained many important achievements. For example, Liu Guoguang, Dai Yuanchen and Zhang Zhuoyuan et al. put forward the idea of "dual-model transformation" of the system model and development model, and the reform strategy of "bi-directional cooperation" based on the cooperation of the two major lines of enterprise reform and price reform;[1] Li Yining et al. put forward the idea of enterprise reform as the main line and the shareholding system as the major form of enterprise reform;[2] Wu Jinglian and Zhou Xiaochuan et al. proposed the idea of "coordinated reform" of comprehensive supporting reform centering on the price reform;[3] Dong Fureng put forward the idea of mixed economy that the socialist economy should be the Eight Treasures Rice,[4] and Wei Xinghua, Hong Yixing and Wei Jie put forward the operating model of planned commodity plan of "plan adjusting the market, market adjusting enterprises",[5] etc. Since October 1987, the State Commission for Restructuring entrusted relevant economic authorities, scientific research institutions, universities and colleges and experts and scholars from a few provinces and municipalities to research the mid-term planning on economic system reform in China from 1988 to 1995, when several comprehensive plans and overall reports of different characteristics were completed, reflecting people's systematic understanding about the goal and model of the economic system reform in that period in a focalized way.[6]

Theories and methods of comparative economics provided important references for us to correctly learn from foreign economic models and made great contribu-tions in freeing China from restraints imposed by conventional theories of the planned economy and exploring the goal and model of economic system reform in China. However, the methods of comparative economics also see significant restrictions. On the one hand, it is based on experiences instead of standards, which compares and summarizes the economic systems existing in history or reality from the empirical perspective but fails to form the general theories of system evolu-tion. On the other hand, this theory is abstract but not practical, because it simpli-fies and schematizes the economic systems formed under different social systems and historical environment. The most serious weakness of western comparative economics is the lack of the scientific idea of materialist conception of history and dialectics, avoiding the comparison between different relations of production of different nature and the fundamental differences of economic laws under different historical stages and social systems, ignoring the profound internal link between the system of ownership of the means of production, specific economic management system and its operating mechanism and abstractly concluding economic systems under different social systems as concentration of power, separation of powers and combination between the power concentration and separation, or as the power mechanism, decision-making mechanism and adjustment mechanism, etc. As these models and factors subject to excessive abstraction and simplification are far from the practical economic life, it is impossible to master the complicated course and internal logic of economic reform and development in China.

(2)   Model of economics in transition: comparison between the gradual reform and radical reform made during the 1990s

Along with the overall transition from the highly concentrated planned economic system to the market economy, the economics in transition emerged as time required. When the Radical Social Changes in Soviet and East Europe occurred in the late 1980s and early 1990s, conventional western economists reached a consensus that the radical reform with macro-economic stabilization, price liberalization and privatization of state-owned enterprises as the core was unique for the transition to the market economy, and people could not leap over one wide gap in only two steps, and the gradual reform could hardly succeed. However, results of practices produced the big surprise. Economists failed to expect that the production may dramatically decline after price liberalization and macro-stabilization, privatization only resulted in benefits of "insiders", organized criminal activities rapidly grew, the Mafia phenomena became even worse, many countries collapsed, and, most surprisingly, China made success in gradual economic reform in China. It demonstrated that mainstream economists' knowledge on and understanding of transition were restricted and were mostly wise after the event.[7] Constant economic growth in China and constant economic decline of the Soviet Union and countries in Eastern Europe made a great contrast. Just as Joseph Stiglitz said, the contrast between the success and failure was so distinct that people would be too irresponsible if not drawing some lessons from it.[8] Along with the process of transition, more and more people agreed with the gradual reform and criticized the radical reform. The comparison between the gradual reform in China and radical reform in the Soviet Union and Eastern Europe had become the focus of economics in transition at that time.

Among the models of economics in transition, representative foreign opinions mainly cover the following three aspects.

The first is the model of neoclassical economics. The neoclassical economists represented by Jeffrey Sachs advocated the Washington Consensus with privatization and liberalization as the core and the radical shock therapy. They believed that the success of gradual reform in China was only an exception, which was only benefited from the favorable initial conditions such as the agriculture-based economic structure and internally loose traditional planned system, so the reform experiences in China had no universal significance. They also emphasized that the gradual reform in China was falling into trouble and encountered a series of so-called challenges and crises of "profound conflicts" as the fundamental privatization and liberalization was not applied.[9]

The second is the Keynesian model. New-Keynesians represented by Joseph Stiglitz believed that incomplete and high-cost information, incomplete capital market and incomplete competition constituted the reality of the market economy, so the neoclassical economics based on Adam Smith's Invisible Hand played a little role in selection of the transition economics and system, and the gradual reform was more useful than the radical reform.[10]Alice H. Amsden and Lance Taylor et al. believed that the visible hand instead of the invisible hand of neoliberalism was more needed in transition to the capitalism, the success of capitalism relied on the system that supported long-term investment and bore risks, and this kind of system could only be constructed by the government.[11]

The third is the model of evolutionism. J. Mcmillan, B. Naughto and some other scholars holding up to evolutionism believed that society was complicated, rationality of people was limited, so reform could only be gradually carried out through experiments, while the most successful reform belonged to countries subject to constant reforms within a longer period instead of countries suffering break between the past and future due to certain economic strategies.[12] Aoki Masahiko et al.[13] believed that the economic system was a complicated system subject to evolution and that different systems might be complementary to each other, and the stronger complementarity required a higher cost for reform; in case of large-scale economic reform, even though the overall direction had been confirmed, the results and process of reform would also be uncertain, so the gradual reform was more applicable.

The three theories noted earlier had no fundamental divergence on the understanding of the nature and the goal of economic transition, while all considered the economic transition as the transition from the socialist planned economy to western capitalist market economy. In terms of the differences, the neoclassical theories advocated the comprehensive one-step process of radical reform; Keynesianism admitted the limitation of the market economy but recognized the significance of interference by the government, and evolutionism unveiled the characteristics of the spontaneous evolution of the capitalist market order. Their common defects lay in that they considered these questions from subjectivism and the world outlook of individualism, lacked the overall and historical investigation on the process of economic transition, regarded the capitalist market economy as the born rational and eternal ideal system and ignored the fundamental differences in the nature and goal between Chinese gradual reform and radical reform in the Soviet Union and Eastern Europe consciously or unconsciously. It should be pointed out that the gradual reform in China was perfecting the fundamental socialist system, while the radical reform in the Soviet Union and Eastern Europe denied the socialist system. Without recognizing the fundamental difference, it is impossible to master the essence of the economic model in China and may be exposed to directional error.

Domestic scholars also conducted in-depth discussions on the transition model in China, while the representative ideas are listed as follows.

Lin Yifu et al. believed that the fundamental cause for the slow development of China before reform was the Catch-up Strategy giving priority to the development of heavy industry, while the key for the rapid development of Chinese economy since reform lay in the reform of the three-in-one traditional economic system, which gave full play to the comparative advantages of resources in China. Meanwhile, the success of reform in China has been guaranteed by the road of the gradual reform of low cost and risk that brought in revenues on a timely basis.[14]

Fan Gang et al. summarized the essence of the gradual reform as the "dual-track transition" and "incremental reform", particularly the rapid development of the non-state economy.[15] Zhang Jun thought that the experience from border reform characterized by the dual-track price was that the state-owned units could master the opportunity for earning profits by responding to the price signal at the border outside the plan, which was quicker than the response to the economic distortion and shortage by state-owned departments subject to sudden privatization.[16]

Zhou Zhenhua believed that the connotation of the economic system reform in China was decided by the structure of the institutional game or the "procedures of reform". The establishment of the "procedures of reform" could be summarized as a dynamic reform goal based on market orientation, flexible selection set of reform for induced incentives and incomplete transactions for institutional transactions. The core running through the whole process should be integration of reform and development.[17]

Qian Yingyi et al. considered that the success of reform in China mainly benefited from the M structure of the traditional system – i.e. the "block-block" structure of multiple layers and regions based on the regional principle. This structure weakened the administrative control, strengthened the market activities and stimulated the development of non-state-owned enterprises.[18] Yang Ruilong believed that during the transition to the market economy, the system transition in China had successively experienced the three stages, the supply orientation, intermediate diffusion and demand orientation, and the local government played the key role in the system transition of intermediate diffusion.[19]

Some other scholars elaborated the characteristics of the mode of economic transition in China from the perspectives of the uncertainty of the reform goal, non-equilibrium of the reform process, non-radicalness of the reform method, significance of spontaneous reform and influence of traditional culture.

Discussions and opinions of Chinese scholars revealed certain experiences and features of the economic transition method in China and enriched the understanding of the process of economic transition.[20] Despite different focuses, these discussions and opinions mostly share the presupposition of the same and confirmed reform goal, and were mainly about the differences of the reform methods. They had major restrictions. First, they failed to deeply investigate on the dialectical relations between the reform process and reform goal but only thought about the transition from the perspective of the methods of marketization. Second, they failed to deeply investigate the close link between the basic socialist system and economic system and ignored that reform was essentially the self-improvement of the socialist system. Third, they had only the abstract and empty economic concept on market but no specific and historical economic concept about the socialist economy.[21]Fourth, they failed to form the theory of economic transition with Chinese characteristics that corresponded to Chinese systems and national conditions and applied more theories of western economics. From these perspectives, the aforementioned opinions had never been able to go fundamentally beyond the model of western economics in transition.

(3)   Model of political economics: discussion on basic characteristics and general significance of the economic model in China since the new century

By entering the new century, the economic system of China has stepped into a new stage. As confirmed by the *Decision of the Central Committee of the Communist Party of China on Several Issues in Perfecting the Socialist Market Economic System* approved in the 3rd Plenary Session of the 16th Communist Party of China (CPC) Central Committee in 2003, the economic system reform in China had acquired significant progress theoretically and practically. The socialist market economic system had been initially established, the basic economic system of keeping public ownership as the mainstay and allowing diverse forms of ownership to develop side by side had been confirmed, and the opening-up pattern of all aspects, broad area and multiple levels had been basically formed.[22] In 2013, the 3rd Plenary Session of the 18th CPC Central Committee formulated the blueprint to deepen the economic system reform in an all-around way for the new stage and pointed out that the overall goal of comprehensively deepening reform was to improve and develop the socialist system with Chinese characteristics, promote the modernization of the national governance system and capability, form the mechanism with complete system, scientific regulations and efficient operation and attained the more matured and well-shaped system in all aspects. This judgment demonstrates that economic transition in China has completed its major goal and task, and the economic reform has been transferred from the stage with "break" as the core in the 1980s and the stage with "establishment" as the core in the 1990s to the stage with "improvement and shaping" as the core.

After 2007, the in-depth discussion on basic characteristics and general significance of the Chinese model was conducted, which was promoted by three major factors.

First, the report from the CPC 17th National Congress made the scientific summary of the basic experiences of Reform and Opening Up of China, put forward the important judgment of Ten Combinations and gave in-depth elaboration about major characteristics of the Chinese model. The report from the CPC 18th National Congress pointed out that it was necessary to strengthen the confidence in the road, theory and system. As an important theoretical concept, the Chinese model has been incorporated in the contemporary academic discourse system, reaching a new height in the understanding of Chinese experiences, Chinese road and Chinese model.

Second, a great number of documents started to discuss the Chinese model, while the discussion on the Chinese model had stepped from the academic level to the mainstream media;[23] from the reform method to the basic system and development model; from the economic field to the political, cultural and social field; and from the experiences summary to the theoretical improvement and discussion on scientific principles. The attention to the Chinese model has been significantly rising, leading to deeper understanding and a great number of achievements.

Third, the global financial and economic crisis triggered by American subprime crisis has still been developing, while the initial financial crisis has been expanded to the economic crisis, political crisis, social crisis and institutional crisis. The in-depth analysis of crises started to lead people to reflect about and criticize the capitalist system. The socialist development road and system model with Chinese characteristics have shown their special advantage in the response to crises, which further causes people's concern and thinking about Chinese model.

In the face of the new situation and tasks, people gradually get rid of the way of thinking of economics in transition and attempt to draw general theories and experiences on economic development and system evolution based on practices in China. The model of economics in transition is being replaced by the model of political economics. As the science that links the productivity and superstructure and researches on the social relation of production and its laws in economic motion, the Marxist political economics shows the fundamental characteristic fundamentally different to the western mainstream economics. Based on fundamental natures, including the world outlook and methodology based on dialectical materialism and historical materialism, the political stand that serves the interests of the proletariat and the broad masses of the people, and the economic analysis system with the mutual effect between the productivity and relation of production as the core, Marxist political economics provides scientific ideological guidance for realization of construction of socialism and communism in the future. Following outstanding features can be seen when the model of Marxist political economics is applied to the understanding of and research on the economic model in China.

First, it attaches more importance to the institutional characteristics of the Chinese model. Wang Zhenzhong et al. applied the Marxist analysis method of the double basic structure of the economic and social form to study the transition of China from two perspectives: the system of relations of production and the system of relations of change, and divided the process of economic transition to two different aspects, the transition from the planned economy to the market economy and the selection of the basic economic system.[24] As pointed out by Cheng Enfu, the evident institutional characteristic that distinguishes the Chinese model from other models lay in the "four major style" system of economic development, the diversified ownership system with public ownership as the main body, the multifactor distribution system with labor as the major factor, the multistructure market system guided by the government and the multidirection opening system oriented on its own efforts.[25]

Second, it pays more attention to the essential connection between the Chinese model and the socialism with Chinese characteristics. As expressly pointed out by Cheng Enfu, the Chinese model is the realization form of the essence of socialism in China.[26] Hu Jun et al. pointed out that the Chinese model was the socialist road with Chinese characteristics, while the key to success was the leadership of the Communist Party of China, dominant role of the public ownership, guiding role of the government and effective use of the market.[27] Qin Xuan and Xu Chongwen et al. emphasized that the Chinese model was the product where our Party combined the universal truth of Marxism and specific practices of China, led our own way and built the socialism with Chinese characteristics.[28] As pointed out by Liu Guoguang, the reason that China could well cope with crises is that we were still holding up to the socialist model with Chinese characteristics.[29]

Third, it pays more attention to the development dimension of the Chinese model. After entering the new century, the understanding of the Chinese model has focused more on development. Chinese model has been regarded as the development model in China in many occasions. How to realize scientific development has become the main topic of economic development in the new period and how to realize the transition of the method of economic development has become the main line for economic development in the new period. The study on the speed, quality, structure and driving force for economic development in China has been taken seriously, and the explanation of the miracle of economic growth in China and the appraisal on the experiences and significance of the development model of China have drawn increasingly wider attention from domestic and foreign academic circle.

Fourth, it attaches more importance to the overall historical structure of the Chinese economic model. More and more people realize that it is necessary to understand and master the connotation of the Chinese model from an overall view and master the overall characteristics of Chinese economic model based on the economic, political, cultural, social and historical organic connections, and it cannot be interpreted in a separate way.[30] More and more people realize that it shall not split the internal connection between the first three decades and second three decades of New China or the profound connection between the contemporary development of China and history and traditions. Some scholars emphasize that the Chinese model is practically about the theoretical explanation on the success of the People's Republic of China in the 60 years and the basis of the Chinese model is the continuity of Chinese civilization.[31]

Fifth, it attaches more importance to the worldwide influence of the Chinese model. As China is involved in the process of economic globalization and along with the increasingly close connection between the Chinese economy and world economy, people begin to explore the historical significance of the Chinese model and the profound influence of the changes to the world order, through the historical evolution of the world system.[32] The rise of the Chinese model has caused people's review on the dependence theory that whether the economic development in China has explored the successful road for independent development or would fall into the trouble of dependent development and repeat the dark future of dependent development.[33] Increasing importance has been attached to influence of the Chinese model on the evolution direction of the human society, development road of developing countries and the future of socialism worldwide.

The aforementioned five new characteristics in the understanding of and research on the Chinese model reflect the dialectical relations of historical materialism and Marxist political economics between the productivity and relations of production, economic base and superstructure, history and logic and theories and practices and represent the historical process of socialist development with Chinese characteristics. It clearly shows that the understanding and research of the academic circle about the Chinese economic model has gone beyond the constricted horizon, value bias and mindset of western mainstream economics and the model of political economics is becoming and will definitely become the main guiding model for the academic circle to understand and research on Chinese economic model.

II.   Major characteristics of Chinese economic model

By now, summary of basic characteristics of Chinese economic model is made based on following different perspectives, first, the basic system; second, the economic system; third, the development road; fourth, the transition method; and fifth, globalization. Practically, these different perspectives have indispensable relation with each other and are indispensable. Among them, the basic system, particularly the basic economic system, plays the key role as the core. According to Marxist political economics, the economic base determines the superstructure, while in the economic base, the basic economic system functions as the core. The basic economic system, referring to the ownership of the means of production and its Constitution determines the essential characteristics of the relations of production of a society; determines every link from production, distribution, exchange to consumption; determines the economic system and road of economic development of the society; and, fundamentally, determines the essence of the superstructure including the political system and ideology of a society. Therefore, it is only possible to accurately master the essence and internal logic of the Chinese economic model by starting from the basic economic system. We can think of it in this way: the Chinese economic model is practically the deployment or realization of the basic economic system of China in the process of reform, development and opening in reality, while its major characteristics could be summarized as the following aspects.

(1)   Basic economic system of keeping public ownership as the mainstay of the economy and allowing diverse forms of ownership to develop side by side

After the foundation of New China, we have established the socialist system based on the public ownership through the socialist transformation. Since Reform and Opening Up, China has gradually confirmed on the basic economic system at the primary stage of socialism of keeping public ownership as the mainstay and allowing diverse forms of ownership to develop side by side. Its major content can be summarized as follows: unswervingly consolidating and developing public-owned economy; unswervingly encouraging, supporting and guiding the development of non-public-owned economy; insisting on equal protection of property rights and forming the new pattern of fair competition and mutual promotion of economies of diversified ownership; deepening reform of state-owned enterprises and forming the modern enterprise system and enterprise operating system adapting to the market economic requirements; optimizing the layout and structure of state-owned economies and enhancing the vigor, control and influence of state-owned economies; stabilizing and constantly improving the rural bilayer operating mechanism based on household contractual management and combination of centralization and decentralization for long term; establishing the modern property right system of clear ownership, rights and responsibilities, strict protection and smooth flow; and developing the mixed-ownership economy on the basis of the modern property right system. Reform of ownership and property right system conducted based on the earlier contents has acquired outstanding achievements in practices and great innovation in theories. It not only insists on the basic principles of scientific socialism but also endows with distinct Chinese characteristics based on practices in China and features of the age; not only invigorates the public-owned economy but also promoted the common development of economies of diversified ownership. As demonstrated by Chinese experiences, the opinion that believes public-owned economy must be inefficient and contractionary to the market economy is not reasonable. The dominant role of the public ownership guarantees the essence of socialism of the market economy and is beneficial for constant, stable and coordinated economic development and realization of the common prosperity of the society. Common development of economies of diversified ownership is favorable to giving full play to the role of different production factors and arousing people's initiative. The establishment of and confirmation on the basic economic system at the primary stage of socialism lays the solid foundation for socialist development with Chinese characteristics. This basic economic system provides great support for China to own relatively strong comprehensive national power and an important international position, to keep constant and stable development among the fierce international competition, to maintain the basic stability of society despite the fierce reform and to withstand the test of major emergencies such as the radical social changes in the Soviet Union and Eastern Europe and East Asia Financial Crisis at the end of the 20th century, the earthquake in 2008 and the financial tsunami.

(2) New style market economic system combined with the basic socialist system – i.e., the socialist market economic system

The goal of the economic system reform in China is to establish the socialist market economic system. The socialist market economy is the new style of the market economy that combines with the basic socialist system. The key to success of economic reform in China lies in the new relation of mutual compatibility and mutual promotion in the basic socialist system particularly between the public-owned economy and market economy. In this new relation, the basic socialist system is given the new meaning and presents the new vigor, and the market economy is given the new feature and reflects the requirements of the basic socialist system. From Chinese practices, it can be seen that the approaches and methods for the combination of the basic socialist system and market economy mainly consist of the following aspects: establish new forms and systems of public ownership that adapt to the market economy and promote the common development of economies of diversified ownership; insist on the dominant role of the public ownership, give play to the leading role of the state-owned economies and strengthen the reform of state-owned enterprises; establish the income distribution system in which distribution according to work is dominant and multiple forms of distribution coexist combining efficiency and equality; generate the unified and open modern market system of orderly competition; establish and improve the macro-control system under guidance by the plan and based on the market; establish and improve the social security system; establish the perfect legal system that adapts to the market economy; establish the new style of social administration system that adapts to the market economy; forms the open economic system of internal and external linkage, mutual benefits, security and efficiency; and constantly improve the Party and the government's capability to control the socialist market economy. Therefore, the organic combination of the basic socialist system and the market economy can be considered as the goal, the essence, the feature and the experience of the economic reform in China. In terms of characteristics of economic operation, the market economic system formed since Reform and Opening Up in China is a kind of market economic system of a socialist power with market adjustment as the basis, government adjustment as the guidance, economic development as the goal and institutional transition as the background, and is a government-guided market economic model that perfectly integrates the plan-oriented adjustment and market-oriented adjustment, centralization of authority and decentralization, direct adjustment and indirect adjustment, supply management and demand management, short-term goal and long-term goal and total equilibrium and structure optimization. This market economic system shows significant differences with the market economic systems of advanced capitalist countries and with the market economic systems of other developing countries and countries in transition. Again, demonstrated by Chinese experiences, the powerful government interference constitutes an indispensable key factor for realization of modernization in developing countries as well as the essential characteristic of the socialist system. The liberal idea of "big market and small government" and "the weaker government control, the better" is completely unreliable.

(3)   *Scientific development road with new industrialization and institutional innovation as the driving force*

Development is the absolute principle and the top priority of the Party in governing and rejuvenating the country. The most attracting feature of the Chinese model is the miracle of high-speed economic growth by nearly 10% for 30 consecutive years. Then, how is the miracle of Chinese economic growth acquired? Domestic and foreign scholars have made explanations from many aspects, such as the broad market demands, stable political environment, high saving rate and investment rate, human resources of low-cost, efficient government interference, market-oriented economy, foreign trade and use of foreign capitals, technical progress and transformation of the dual structure. Fundamentally, the driving force of the constant and rapid growth of Chinese economy is the constantly deepening new industrialization and institutional innovation. Mutual promotion between industrialization and informatization and the overall innovation of the economic and social system, on the one hand, inspire the constant increase of investment of resources including capitals and labors and increasing demands, and, on the other hand, promote the constant improvement of the efficiency of resources allocation and constant deepening economic innovation. This is a kind of structural or revolutionary economic growth jointly driven by the structural transition, technical progress and institutional innovation. The new industrialization and institutional innovation will maintain to be the basic factor that drives the growth in a long period, providing the constant and stable driving force for economic growth in China. This is exactly the so-called secret of the Chinese economic miracle. The most important achievement and the most valuable experience of the Chinese economic model lies in that it starts from practices in China and explores and forms the development theories, development strategies and development road that meets Chinese characteristics, most importantly the scientific outlook on development, strategy of "three-step economic development" and construction of a well-off society in an all-around way, as well as the road of economic development that reflects the requirements of scientific development including the new industrialization road with Chinese characteristics, rural modernization road with Chinese characteristics, independent innovation road with Chinese characteristics, urbanization road with Chinese characteristics and regional development road with Chinese characteristics. These achievements reflect the objective requirements of socialism with Chinese characteristics on development and open up the broader and brighter future for economic development in China.

(4) *Independent opening-up strategy*

Since Reform and Opening Up, China has established the basic national policy on opening up; adopted the active, gradual and controlled approach and realized the historical turn from the close and semi-close status to the overall opening by establishing special economic zones; opened the coastal area, riverside area, border area and inland area; joined the World Trade Organization; and lead the path from large-scale "bringing in" to "going out" in large steps. The model of opening up China mainly reveals following characteristics. First, it plans for the domestic and international situation at the same time and insists on the opening-up strategy of mutual benefits; combines "bringing in" and "going out"; makes full use of the international and domestic market, optimizes the allocation of resources and explores the development room; and promotes reform and development through opening-up. Second, it clarifies the duality and the two development trends of economic globalization. On the one hand, it promotes the rational allocation of world resources, improves development of productivity at different countries and thus benefits people; on the other hand, being the global expansion of capitalist economic relations, it further aggravates the imbalance in allocation of world resources and economic development, widens the gap between development in the south and that in the north, and intensifies the polarization between the rich and poor and environmental deterioration. We select and promote the first kind of trend and warn and control the latter kind of trend. Third, it combines active involvement in economic globalization with independence, places the foothold on China's own strength while insisting on opening up, integrates introduction and opening innovation and use of foreign capitals and accumulations of its own, pays attention to maintain the national sovereignty and economic security, prevents and relieves the attack by international risk and maintains the control of the government on key sectors and areas. We constantly improve our capability in independent innovation, try to build the innovation-oriented country and form the new advantages in international economic cooperation under economic globalization.

(5)   *Gradual transition with socialist market economy as the goal*

In late 1980s and early 1990s, two different paths emerged for the transition from the traditional planned economy to the market economy – i.e. the radical reform in the Soviet Union and Eastern Europe and the gradual reform in China. The success of economic reform in China not only demonstrates to the world that socialism could be combined with the market economy but also enables China to discover the road of gradual reform or the reform method with Chinese characteristics from the practices. Major characteristics of the reform method consist of the following:

- Through combination of reform from top to bottom and reform from bottom to top and based on unified leadership, give full play to the enthusiasm and creation of the basic-level units in institutional innovation.
- Based on dual-track transition, incremental quantity first and preservation of plan for coordination, steadily transit to the market economy by gradually expanding the proportion of market adjustment among the newly increased resources.
- Based on overall coordination, breakthroughs and the overall national plan, realize the overall transition of the economic system by taking the experiences gained from breakthroughs in each department, enterprise and region to the whole area.
- Give consideration to reform, development and stability at the same time, combine the strength of reform and speed of development with the acceptance ability of the society, promote reform and development based on social stability and enhance social stability through reform and development.

- Carry out reform in different steps, proceed in an orderly way, make test before generalization and constantly adjust and improve the specific goal and thinking of reform based on demands of practices and development of understanding.

The goal decides the method, while the method is generated based on the goal. We shall not abstractly discuss the method of reform without considering the attribute and the goal of the Reform. Economic reform in China applying the gradual method is fundamentally decided by the special reform goal of the socialist market economy.

First, the socialist market economy is the one combined with the basic socialist system. The goal of reform is not to fundamentally deny the basic socialist system but to endow the basic socialist system with new vigor through institutional innovation to overcome weaknesses of the traditional planned economic system. This fundamental essence of economic reform in China determines that its method and process would be moderate and gradual. The new and the old system are not opposite to each other, but show evident continuity and succession. The transition between them needs to experience many specific stages, passes many intermediate links, and adopts many intermediate forms.

Second, China is currently in the primary stage of socialism, where the market development and role of the market system is not only restricted by the social system but also restricted by the stage of economic development. In the long term, it will be subject to restraints such as rough division of work, simple structure, inhibited information delivery, weak infrastructure and large gap between the urban and rural area. In China, marketization and industrialization and the transition of the system model and transition of the development model are integrated. Therefore, the generation and development of the market economy requires a long historical course, so only the gradual reform is applicable in China.

Third, the socialist market economy is a new kind of market economy, while its specific meaning and form of realization is not transcendental or fixed but is subject to constant changes and development and certain uncertainty. Practically, the reform goal of the socialist market economy was not clarified at first, but was the product of the long-term exploration from the planned economy, commodity economy to the socialist market economy. The establishment of the goal of socialist market economic system reform has not solved all issues on the reform goal, while the socialist market economy already formed still needs constant improvement.

Therefore, the fundamental difference between the gradual reform in China and the radical reform in the Soviet Union and Eastern Europe does not lie in the method and approach of marketization, but lies in the goal and essence of reform. According to Janos Kornai, the difference between the gradual and radical reform is not about the method and speed of transition or the moderate or fierce status of the Reform, but is actually about whether it is a reform or the so-called revolution.[34] The goal of economic reform in China is to improve the socialist system, while the goal of the radical reform in the Soviet Union and

Eastern Europe is to deny the socialist system, which is the fundamental difference between the gradual reform in China and the radical reform in the Soviet Union and Eastern Europe.

The aforementioned characteristics of Chinese economic model constitute an organized whole with intercommunication. In terms of the basic system, the Chinese economic model is keeping public ownership as the mainstay and allowing diverse forms of ownership to develop side by side; from the perspective of the economic system, it presents as the socialist market economic system; regarding the Opening Up to foreign countries, it is the independent opening-up strategy, and, in terms of economic development, it is the road of scientific development. By concentrating these contents of mutual interaction together, it is actually the construction of the socialist economy with Chinese characteristics. The socialism with Chinese characteristics is the core and spirit of the Chinese economic model. The process of generation and development of the Chinese economic model is exactly the process of the generation of the development of theories and practices on the socialist economy with Chinese characteristics.

To understand the basic characteristics of the Chinese economic model, one should first understand the following points. First, the Chinese economic model has been developed based on socialist revolution and construction in the three decades after the foundation of New China. The reform and construction in the first three decades laid the historical material and institutional foundation for the generation of the Chinese economic model, while the practices in the three decades after Reform and Opening Up have formed the basic content and major framework of the Chinese economic model. Second, the core of the Chinese economic model is the basic economic system at the primary stage of socialism, with the major content of promoting marketization, industrialization and opening up based on the socialist system and the theme of developing the socialism with Chinese characteristics. Third, the Chinese economic model incorporates relatively stable universal characteristics but is also a dynamic concept exposed to constant reform and development, which shows different patterns of manifestation in different stages, departments and regions. Fourth, the Chinese economic model reflects the universal laws of economic and social development as well as features of the time, and meanwhile reveals the national features and the basic system of China, making it the new economic model created from the integration of generality and personality.

III. Contradictions and choice faced by the Chinese economic model

Though the Chinese economic model has been formed and acquired remarkable achievements, it still needs further improvement and faces some violent contradictions and serious issues, such as the deteriorated ecological environment, increasing pressure on unemployment, widening gap between the rich and poor, poor independent innovation, backward development of social undertakings, incomplete social security system and serious corruption.

Two totally opposite opinions against the earlier issues are popular in recent years.

The first is the idea of neoliberalism. It believes that the success of reform in China results from the so-called privatization, liberalization and internationalization applied, while the problems in Chinese reform are incurred by insufficient privatization, liberalization and internationalization, too large proportion of the public-owned economy and state-owned economy, too much government interference and social adjustment, weak internalization and backward reform of the political system. It reaches the conclusion that it is necessary to further deepen the reform of marketization, to continue to decrease and cancel the government interference and social adjustment, to realize complete privatization of state-owned enterprises, to facilitate the steps to gear into the international economy gradually introduce the so-called democratic constitutional regime of western style and to lay the political and legal foundation for the role of the free market.

The second idea questions the direction of the market economic reform in China, which is popular among some neo-left scholars in the west, represented by David Harvey, Martin Hart and R. Walker et al.[35] Scholars holding up the opinion believe that reform of marketization leads to the decline of the proportion of state-owned enterprises in China and the rise of the proportion of private enterprises, increasingly unfair distribution of incomes and wealth, increasing dependence of economic expansion on foreign investment and export, increasingly fierce crisis in resources and environment and increasingly prominent class contradictions and increasingly intensified social conflicts. These problems cannot be overcome if no change to the reform direction of the orientation of the market economy and the corresponding ownership and class structure.

The opinions of the western neo-left school and neoliberalism seem like being opposite but are consistent with each other. They both deny the possibility and rationality of the combination of the socialism and the market economy and thus fundamentally deny the value and significance of Chinese economic model. The difference lies in that the neoliberalism denies the socialism, while the western neo-left school denies the market economy. Apparently, they are no new opinions at all, but just repeat the right and "left" doctrine view that places the socialism and the market economy at the opposite positions.

What way will the Chinese economic model lead? Will it be overthrown and started all over again or be further improved? This is the major choice in front of us. For this question, the report from the CPC 18th National Congress, the decision of the 3rd Plenary Session of the 18th CPC Central Committee and series of speeches made by the General Secretary Xi Jinping have constituted the complete elaboration to reply to this question that unswervingly takes the road of socialism with Chinese characteristics and rejects both the old and rigid closed-door policy, and any attempt to abandon socialism takes an erroneous path. General Secretary Xi Jinping has emphasized many times that "China is a big country where the subversive error is not allowed". The strategic focus and bottom-line thinking are required for issues related to the road and direction. The strategic focus means to unswervingly insist on taking the road of socialism with Chinese characteristics, while the bottom-line thinking means to hold up to the bottom line of the socialist system with Chinese characteristics and resolutely oppose any attempt to change the essence of the socialist system. It expressly tells everyone that Chinese model needs further self-improvement and development instead of self-negation and scraping and starting all over again.

The first is to improve the economic system. Acquire decisive achievements in the reform of main fields and key links, form the mechanism with complete system, scientific regulations and efficient operation and attain the more matured and well-shaped system at all aspects by 2020. The key is to improve the basic economic system of keeping public ownership as the mainstay and allowing diverse forms of ownership to develop side by side, improve the distribution system of keeping the labor-oriented distribution as the mainstay and allow diverse forms of distribution methods, prevent the privatization and polarization and ensure that people can share the results of reform and development.

The second is to improve the economic system. The core issue is to handle the relation between the government and market well, give full play to the decisive role of the market in the allocation of resources and the greater role of government, focus on solving the problems of the incomplete market system, too much government interference and insufficient supervision and promote the vigor of the market. The responsibilities and role of the government are mainly maintaining the macro-economic stability, strengthening and optimizing the public service, guaranteeing the fair competition, intensifying the market supervision, maintaining the market order, promoting sustainable development, promoting common prosperity and making up the market failure.

The third is to improve the method of economic development; transfer the foothold of development to improvement of quality and benefits; push the economic development to rely more on internal demands, particularly the consumption demands, on the modern service sector and strategic emerging industries on technical progress; improvement of laborer's quality and management innovation on conservation of resources and circular economy, and on coordinated interaction between the development of the urban and rural areas; and constantly enhance the reserve strength for long-term development.

The fourth is to improve the opening-up strategy; improve the open economic system of mutual benefits, multiple equilibrium, security and efficiency; promote the transition of the Opening Up to structure optimization, depth exploration and benefit improvement; actively participate in economic globalization; insist on the policy of independence and self-reliance; hold up to, maintain and enhance national interests; place a foothold on relying our own strength; protect the economic and financial security of the country; improve the ability of independent innovation; and form the new advantages in participating international economic cooperation and competition under economic globalization.

The fifth is to improve the method of economic reform, realize the dialectical unity of moving steadily and strengthening the design of top layer, attach more importance to overall design when deepening the Reform, make overall plan and promote improvement systematically, give more overall consideration and pay attention to democratic decision making and coordinate different types of interests and relations during reform. More importance shall to attached to mutual promotion, favorable interaction, overall promotion and key point solution of all reforms, thus to generate the strong resultant force to promote Reform and Opening Up.

In conclusion, the Chinese economic model has revealed its extreme superiority and strong vitality in practices. Only by admitting it and enhancing our confidence in theories, road and system, we can take over from the past and set a new course for the future and acquire greater achievements. The opinion believing that the economy has stopped development and is about to collapse, and the model needs to be overthrown and replaced by the radical reform does not comply with the facts. On the other hand, we shall see that Chinese economic model is not a fixed thing, but the course of rich and vigorous historical creation that keeps up with the times. We must proceed from reality, constantly solve and overcome all disputes and problems in the real economy, constantly enrich and improve the connotation of the Chinese model, endow it with the new vigor and creation and thus broaden the road of socialism with Chinese characteristics.

IV. Significance of Chinese economic model: universality and particularity

Is the Chinese economic model a special case or does it have the universal significance? People have a different understanding about its universality. People who deny its universality believe that success of China mainly benefits from a series of favorable initial conditions, so the experiences of Chinese reform have no universal significance but are only the product of the special environment. People who recognize the universality believe that the Chinese reform has led a successful road of low cost and risk and spontaneous benefits, and as the traditional economic system, as well as its weaknesses, are the same in countries exposed to reform, the road of reform shall be consistent. Therefore, the experiences of Chinese reform are universal instead of being unique. Scholars holding up this idea also believe that the similar conditions decide the applicability of theories, and as developing countries share similar conditions, challenges and opportunities, the theoretical innovation of China not only helps China better understand and decide Chinese problems and makes contributions to the realization of the Chinese dream of the great rejuvenation of the Chinese nation but also provides reference to economic development of other developing countries.[36]

The economic model of China shall be first considered as the product of the special national conditions of China, which is closely linked to the socialist road with Chinese characteristics and the basic system of China. In addition, the special initial conditions, special historical and cultural traditions, special reform route and even the special style of the leadership all constitute the important factors for the establishment of the Chinese economic model. Going on our own way is the fundamental experience for the success of Chinese revolution as well as the fundamental experience for the success of reform and development in China. Any dogmatic approach that mechanically copies theories and experiences of other countries would definitely fail to the diversified and vigorous practices in reform and development of China. Meanwhile, the model and experience successful in China are not necessarily applicable to any time and any country. The market economic systems of different times and different countries share similarity and show difference. There is no abstract market economy that is applicable to any time and country. Only the model of market economic development established in the real and historical market economic environment and the market economic system is the vigorous economic model.

Someone may say that market economy shall be universal worldwide and has no difference in any country and region no matter in the socialist or capitalist environment, so the market economy with Chinese characteristics is impossible to exist. However, the fact speaks the other way. The market economy is not a certain facility or tool that could survive without the specific social structure or that could be moved around the different institutional environment and historical conditions. On the contrary, the market economic systems in different historical stages and social structures share both similarities and differences. The classical market economy is different with the modern market economy; the model of UK and America is not the model in Northern Europe, and the model in East Asia presents its unique characteristics. When developing the market economy and realizing the industrialization, compared with other countries, China was encountered the following special social and historical conditions: the long and profound historical and cultural traditions, socialist economic and political system, dual transition of industrialization and informatization, large population and relatively scarce resources, relatively backward position in the world capitalist system and vast land and strong differences between different regions, etc. Therefore, the Chinese economic model reflects both of the general laws of economic modernization and market economic development and the special systems, national conditions and requirements of the historical stages in China. It respects general laws and incorporates the innovative spirit, has its particularity and universal significance and is national and meanwhile international.

The emphasis on Chinese characteristics does not mean that the Chinese economic model is only a special case of the accidental phenomenon. The generality is contained in the personality, while the particularity contains the universality. The formation and development of the market economy bears objective and universal laws, while the Chinese experiences and models necessarily contain certain general laws and meanings. The experience and model of economic development in China has broadened the vision of economics research, enriched the understanding about the laws of market economic development and deepened the recognition of the laws of economic development and institutional transition, which have been accepted by more and more people. Though the so-called Beijing Consensus cannot be considered as a good theoretical and authentic interpretation, it reflects people's hope to improve Chinese experiences.[37] Zou Zhizhuang's idea is also representative. According to his book *Economic Transition in China*, in addition to the methodology, the researches on the economic transition in China provide six subjects about the essence of economics: private ownership does not necessary generate the management efficiency; the market incentives may not be abundant for the rapid economic development; the form of government is non-related to the speed of economic development; different economic systems could serve for the market economy; political feasibility is an important factor for economic transition; the bureaucratic economic system under the central plan can hardly be removed.[38]

In the development course of human history, the Chinese nation has not been and should never be the imitator or follower of theories of other countries, but shall make certain invention, creation and contribution. Chinese economic model provides an enlightenment to people about how to make factors seemingly opposite to each other complement, integrate, penetrate, enhance and develop each other, including the public and private ownership, efficiency and equality, government and market, freedom and harmony, decentralization and centralization, economy and society, development and stability, traditions and modernization, independence and globalization, new system and old system and so on. In conclusion, the fundamental significance of the Chinese model lies in theoretically defeating the skopos theory of the capitalist modernization, starting from distinguishing industrialization, modernization, marketization and capitalization, reaching the conclusion that the transition of modernization and marketization is not necessary to base on the standard of capitalist industrialization and market economy, challenge the capitalist ideology of superiority and universality and realize the historical integration of socialism and market economy.[39] The integration itself is the characteristic, the creation.

As is known to all, economists hold up to diversified opinions on the relationship between the government and market, leading to the persistent antagonistic argument between the economic liberalism and state interventionism and forming many ideas such as the Free Market Theory, State Regulation Theory, State Development Theory, Market Control Theory, Market Friendly View and Theory of Development-Oriented Government. However, any idea of them can hardly accurately explain Chinese experiences and reality. Due to relatively similar historical and cultural traditions and development stage, the Chinese economic model owns relatively obvious characteristics of so-called development-oriented government.[40] However, even compared to general development-oriented government, the relation between the government and market in China presents more new characteristics. First, the relation between the government and market is not a single form, but diversified form, presenting different combinations in different sectors, enterprises and fields. For example, the relation at the coastal area is different from that of the inland, the rural area is different from the urban area, the agriculture is different from the industry and the state-owned enterprises are different from non-state-owned enterprises. Second, the relation between the government and market is not fixed but exposed to constant changes. Different models have emerged in different development stages, such as the model with the planned economy as the mainstay and market regulation as the complementary approach, the model of planned commodity economy and the model of the socialist market economic system, while the socialist market economic system shows different characteristics in different stages. Third, the relation between the government and market is reflected by multiple dimensions, such as the relationship between economy, politics, culture and society, between the macro- and micro-view and between the productivity and relations of production. For example, scientific development, social harmony, political motivation, plan coordination, overall plan, macro-control, micro-regulation, institutional innovation and state-owned assets management all reflect the economic function of the government. Fourth, the relation between the central and local government plays a special and important role. The local government is a certain level of administrative organization and bears the role similar to entrepreneur, thus leading to the complicated structure of the relation between the government and market and becoming an important factor that affects reform and development of China. Fifth, the relation between the government and market has a close relation to the socialist economic and political system and reflects the requirements of the basic socialist economic and political system. The innovative behaviors and ideas on the relationship between the government and market in the Chinese model greatly inspire the development of economic theories and practices. We believe that along with the development and expanding influence of Chinese economic model, people's exploration on the universal significance of Chinese economic model is constantly strengthening and deepening.

In order to strengthen and deepen the understanding of the Chinese experience and model, it is necessary to stay alert against the principle and even the knowledge system of western mainstream economics and stay conscious of their restrictions and bias. Currently, it is particularly necessary to break this new form of dogmatism and obscurantism. These ideas believe that there is only one kind of economics worldwide – i.e. the western mainstream economics, which is "scientific" and "universal" without any restriction on nation or border – and the so-called Chinese economics and Chinese economic model do not exist, but only the application and promotion of western economics and western economic model in China. This kind of idea is wrong. First, western economics consists of numerous theories and schools, while the position and influence of these theories and schools have been constantly changing along with historical development. The modern western neoclassical economics highly recognized by many people is actually only one branch among numerous economics schools and is never the universal and eternal truth. Second, as with the development of human civilization, economics is proposed by people from different countries, different times and different groups based on their own special environment, experiences and knowledge background, which is the result of mutual exchange, collision and integration of different ideas and theories. Therefore, development of economics is absolutely not the patent of certain countries or certain people. Third, development of China is realized under historical conditions and international and domestic environment different to the industrialization of western countries, and shall not mechanically copy the western model and experience. Finally, any economic theory is established based on certain reality and inevitably reflects the interest trend, historical experiences, values, cultural background and way of thinking of the theory producer. The mechanical copy of western economic theories and development model does not help understanding of Chinese road and model, but will make us the slave to the new dogmatism or neo-Obscurantism who lacks the confidence and capability in independent development and independent innovation. Huntington Samuel frankly admitted, "The concept of universal civilization is the unique product of western civilization".

> At the end of the 20th century, the concept of the universal civilization was beneficial for the west to culturally rule other societies and for the societies to simulate western practices and systems. The universalism is the ideology that the west makes use of to deal with non-western societies.[41]

The great rejuvenation of the Chinese nation will be necessarily accompanied by the prosperity of theories, and China shall make greater contributions to human. We shall summarize experiences from practices of China, abstract ideas, innovate on theories and develop the independent and original economic theories that adapt to the Chinese economic model, to live up to our age and our nation.

The economic model of China has explored a new road and presented a new possibility for developing countries to step to modernization, develop market economy and involve globalization and meanwhile brings about the hope for human progress and rejuvenation of socialism. As stated in the article of *Commemoration on Mr. Sun Yat-sen* by Mao Zedong in 1956, "China shall make greater contributions to human but we have failed to make our due contributions in a very long period, and we feel ashamed for this".[42] In 1987 when Deng Xiaoping met a foreign leader, he predicted,

> By the middle of the next century, we will attain the level of the moderately developed countries. By reaching the goal, firstly, we accomplished a very hard and difficult task; secondly, we made real contributions to human; and thirdly, it revealed the superiority of socialism.

"We are not only leading the Third World occupying over 3/4 population of the world to another road, but demonstrating that socialism is the route one must take and socialism is superior to capitalism".[43] Currently, when Chinese people are making great progress in building the prosperous, democratic, civilized and harmonious modernized socialist country courageously with constant innovation in practices, we can say that the success of the Chinese model is the greater contribution that the Chinese nation donates to the development of human civilization.

Notes

1 Chief editor Liu Guoguang, *Research on Models of Economic System Reform in China*, China Social Sciences Press, Edition 1988.
2 Li Yining, *Thinking on Economic Reform in China*, China Expectation Press, Edition 1989.
3 Wu Jinglian and Zhou Xiaochuan et al., *Overall Design of the Economic System Reform in China*, China Expectation Press, Edition 1988.
4 Dong Fureng, *Research on Economic System Reform*, Economic Science Press, Edition 1994.

 5 Wei Xinghua, Hong Yinxing, and Wei Jie, "Planned Adjustment Orientation and Restricted Market Adjustment", *Economic Study*, 1987, 1st Issue, Page 57–61.
 6 Division of Comprehensive Planning of State Commission for Restructuring, *Big Ideas for Reform of China*, Shenyang Press, Edition 1988.
 7 [Belgium] Gerard Roland, *Transition and Economics*, translated by Zhang Fan and Pan Zuohong, Beijing University Press, Edition 2002.
 8 [US] Joseph Stiglitz, *Where Is the Reform Leading? – On Transition in the Decade*, referring to Hu An'gang and Wang Shaoguang, *Government and Market*, China Planning Press, Beijing, Edition 2000.
 9 Jeffrey Sachs and Wing Woo, "Structural Factor in the Economic Reforms of China, Eastern Europe and Former Soviet Union", *Economy Policy*, Vol. 18, April 1994, Page 102–145.
10 Joseph E. Stiglitz, *Whither Socialism*, Cambridge, MA: The MIT Press, 1994.
11 Allice H. Amsden, Jacek Kochanowicz, and Lance Taylor, *The Market Meets It's Match: Restructuring the Economies of Eastern Europe*, Cambridge, MA: Harvard University Press, 1994.
12 [US] Peter Monle, *Discussion on Radical Economic Reform and Gradual Economic Reform*, referring to Li Xinggeng, Li Zongyu, and Rong Jingben, *Contemporary Foreign Economists Discussing on Market Economy*, CPC Central Party School Press, Edition 1994; J. Mcmillan and B. Naughto, "How to Reform a Planned Economy: Lesson From China", *Oxford Review of Economic Policy*, Vol. 8, 1st Issue, 1992, Page 130–143.
13 [JP] Aoki Masahiko and Ono Masahiro, *Comparison and Analysis of Economic Systems*, translated by Wei Jianing et al., China Development Press, Edition 1999.
14 Lin Yifu, Cai Fang, and Li Zhou, *Chinese Miracle: Development Strategy and Economic Reform*, Shanghai Joint Publishing, Shanghai People's Publishing House, Edition 1994.
15 Fan Gang, *Political Economics Analysis on Gradual Reform*, Shanghai Far East Publishing House, Edition 1996.
16 Zhang Jun, *"Dual-track" Economics, Economic Reform in China (1978–1992)*, Shanghai Joint Publishing, Shanghai People's Publishing House, Edition 1997.
17 Zhou Zhenhua, *System Reform and Economic Growth – Analysis of Chinese Experiences and Model*, Shanghai Joint Publishing, Shanghai People's Publishing House, Edition 1999.
18 Qian Yingyi and Xu Chenggang, "Why the Economic Reform Is Different From Others", *Economic and Social System Comparison*, 1993, 10th Issue, Page 29–40.
19 Yang Ruilong, "Three Stages for System Transition Methods in China", *Economic Research*, 1998, 1st Issue, Page 5–12.
20 During this period, some scholars had realized the decisive role of the reform goal and constitution system in the road of reform. For example, in the book *Road of Transition: Political Economics Analysis of Gradual Reform in China*, the author had put forward an analysis framework of economics in transition based on the overall Marxist political economics model and defined the gradual reform in China as "marketization under restrictions by industrialization and socialist constitution system". However, this kind of opinion was rarely seen at that time. (Refer to Zhang Yu, *Road of Transition: Political Economics Analysis of Gradual Reform in China*, China Social Sciences Publishing House, Edition 1997).
21 Jiang Zemin emphasized, "The word 'socialist' cannot be missing. It is not unnecessary or superfluous; while, on the contrary, it is crucial that it points out the nature of our market economy". (Jiang Zemin, *On Socialist Market Economy*, CPC Archives Publishing House, Edition 2006, Page 202).
22 *Decision of the Central Committee of the Communist Party of China on Several Issues in Perfecting the Socialist Market Economic System*, CPC Central Committee Archives

Research Office, *Collection of Important Archives Since the 16th National People's Congress* (Vol. 1), CPC Central Committee Archives Press, Edition 2005, Page 464.

23 Since 2008, *People's Daily Online*, *People's Tribune*, *Social Sciences in China* and *Economic Perspectives* and some other important media and magazines had published the discussion on the Chinese model.

24 Wang Zhenzhong, *Political Economics Analysis on Transition Economy in China*, China Price Publishing House, Edition 2002.

25 Cheng Enfu, "Characteristics and Connotation of the Economic System of Chinese Model", *Economic Perspectives*, Vol. 1, 2009, 12th Issue, Page 12–23.

26 Cheng Enfu, "Chinese Model: Realization Form of the Essence of Socialism in China", *Social Sciences in China Press*, January 11, 2011.

27 Hu Jun and Han Dong, Essence, "Characteristics and Challenges of the Chinese Model", *Review of Political Economics*, 2010, 4th Issue.

28 Qin Xuan, "Analysis of the Concept of 'Chinese Model'", *Frontier*, 2010, 2nd Issue, Page 5–10, 159; Xu Chongwen, "Several Issues on How to Understand the Chinese Model", *Marxism Research*, 2010, 2nd Issue, Page 28–32.

29 Liu Guoguang, "Chinese Model Renders us the Hope to Realize Rejuvenation as the First", *Red Flag Manuscript*, 2009, 11th Issue, Page 39.

30 Zhao Jianying and Wu Bo, *Discussion on the Chinese Model*, China Social Sciences Publishing House, Edition 2010.

31 Pan Wei, *Chinese Model: Explanation on the 60 Years of the People's Republic*, Central Compilation & Translation Press, Edition 2009.

32 Representative work includes [US] Giovanni Arrighi, *Adam Smith in Beijing*, translated by Lu Aiguo, Huang Ping, Xu Anjie, Social Science Academic Press, Edition 2009, Page 10.

33 [Netherlands] Andrew Fisher, "Is China Subject to Latin Americanization? Balance Between Power and Dependence of China Among the Global Imbalance", *Review of Political Economics*, Vol. 1, 2010, 4th Issue, Page 36–53; Lu Di, "World Development Crisis and 'Chinese Model'", *Review of Political Economics*, Vol. 1, 2010, 4th Issue, Page 24–35.

34 "Revolution" mentioned by János Kornai refers to the overall privatization of the public owned economies. János Kornai, *Highway and Byways: Studies on Reform and Post-communist Transition*, Cambridge, MA: The MIT Press, 1995.

35 Refer to D. Harvey, *A Brief History of Neoliberalism*, Oxford, NY: Oxford University Press, 2005, Page 120–151; Martin Hart-Landsberg and Paul Burkett, *China and Socialism: Market Reform and Class Struggle*, New York: Monthly Review Press, 2005; R. Walker and D. Buck, "The Chinese Road, Cities in the Transition to Capitalism", *New Left Review*, Vol. 46, July/August, 2007, Page 39–66.

36 Refer to Lin Yifu, Cai Fang and Li Zhou, *Chinese Miracle: Development Strategy and Economic Reform*, Shanghai Joint Publishing, Shanghai People's Publishing House, Edition 1994; Lin Yifu, Cai Fang, and Li Zhou, *Chinese Miracle: Development Strategy and Economic Reform* (enlarged edition), Truth & Wisdom Press, Shanghai Joint Publishing, Shanghai People's Publishing House, Edition 2014.

37 [US] Joshua Cooper Ramo, *Beijing Consensus*; Huang Ping and Cui Zhiyuan, *China and Globalization: Washington Consensus or Beijing Consensus*, Social Science Academic Press, Edition 2005.

38 Zou Zhizhuang, *Economic Transition in China*, China Renmin University Press, Edition 2005.

39 Lin Chun, "Discussion on the 'Chinese Model'", *Review of Political Economics*, Vol. 1, 2010, 4th Issue, Page 64–72.

40 The original model of the development-oriented government is the so-called East Asian model, and its major characteristics include the follows: high government interference to the economy, promoting economic development by formulating the development

strategy, planning and policies such as supporting industries, etc., basic consistency between the political elite and economic elite on development, and cooperation between the government and society, etc.

41 [US] Huntington Samuel, *Civilization Conflicts and Reconstruction of the World Order*, translated by Zhou Qi et al., Xinhua Publishing House, Edition 1998, Page 55 and 56.

42 Mao Zedong, *Commemoration on Mr. Sun Yat-sen*, November 12, 1956, Vol. 7 of *Collections of Mao Zedong*, People's Publishing House, Edition 1999, Page 157.

43 Deng Xiaoping, *Socialism Shall Get Rid of Poverty*, April 26, 1987, Vol. 3 of *Collections of Deng Xiaoping*, People's Publishing House, Edition 1994, Page 225.

3 Theories and practices on socialist market economy

The Communist Party of China officially confirmed on the goal of reform as the socialist market economic system in 1992, since when the socialism with Chinese characteristics stepped into a brand-new phase. In over two decades, we have been committed to perfecting the socialist economic system, fundamentally liberated and developed social productive forces and acquired remarkable achievements. As proved by practices, the establishment of the socialist market economic system is a major theoretical contribution that has provided the institutional guarantee to correctly solve major issues related to the overall situation of socialism.

I. Historical process of establishment and improvement of socialist market economy

After the establishment of the socialist system, it is a major theoretical and practical problem to choose the economic system. The core of the issue lies in how to view the status and the role of the market mechanism under socialist conditions.

Based on profound analysis of the basic social conflicts of capitalism, Karl Marx and Friedrich Engels put forward that once the society occupied the means of production, the commodity production was eliminated, and the society would regulate on all productions as planned. After the foundation of New China, according to this theory and Chinese practices, China had gradually established the highly concentrated planned economy, having formed the relatively complete independent industrial system and national economic system in a short time and laid the political and economic basis for the development of contemporary China. However, the highly concentrated planned economic system is exposed to weaknesses including no clear separate responsibilities of government and enterprise and ignorance of the commodity production and the role of the market, etc., which severely restrained the development of productive forces.

Since the time of Reform and Opening Up, the Communist Party of China has gained a deepening understanding of the market mechanism. The 3rd Plenary Session of the 11th Central Committee of the Party proposed to follow economic laws and attach importance to the law of value; the 12th National Congress put forward the idea of "leading role of the planned economy and the supplementary role of market regulation"; the 3rd Plenary Session of the 12th Central Committee of the Party put forward that "the socialist economy is the planned commodity economy based on public ownership"; the 13th National Congress put forward that "the planned commodity economic system should integrate plan and market". In early 1992, Deng Xiaoping pointed out in the Talks in the South, "The proportion of plan and market is not the fundamental difference between socialism and capitalism, while the plan and market are both economic means".[1] In June 1992, based on the spirit of Deng Xiaoping's Talks in the South, Jiang Zemin proposed the concept of "socialist market economic system". In October of the same year, the Report of the 14th National Congress of CPC expressly pointed out, "The goal of economic system reform in China is to establish the socialist market economic system" and "enable the market to play the fundamental role in allocation of resources under the macro-control of the socialist government", which symbolized the great breakthrough in understanding and practices of the economic system reform of our Party.

As the experiences and lessons from domestic and foreign socialist construction summarized by our Party and the result of the increasingly deepening understanding about laws and reform of socialist construction, the establishment of the reform goal of the socialist market economic system had fundamentally eliminated the confusion in theories and practices since Reform and Opening Up, correctly solved major issues related to the overall situation and direction of socialist modernization construction and realized the historical breakthrough of Reform and Opening Up. On the basis, the 3rd Plenary Session of the 14th Central Committee of the Party had made the *Decision of the CPC Central Committee on Several Issues Related to Construction of the Socialist Market Economic System* and pushed forward the overall foundation of the socialist market economic system; the 3rd Plenary session of the 16th Central Committee made the *Decision of the CPC Central Committee on Several Issues Related to Improvement of the Socialist Market Economic System* and pushed forward the constant improvement of the socialist market economic system; the 17th National Congress of CPC further emphasized improving the socialist market economic system, facilitating reform in important areas and key links and building the vigorous, efficient and open system and mechanism that is beneficial to scientific development; the 18th National Congress pointed out is was necessary to apply greater political courage and wisdom to grasp opportunities to deepen reform in important sectors, facilitate improvement of the socialist market economic system, build the system of complete system, science and efficient operation and realize the more mature and defined system.

Currently, under the socialist market economic system, Reform and Opening Up is being implemented in an all-around way, the basic economic system of keeping public ownership as the mainstay and allowing diverse forms of ownership to develop side by side is constantly improved, and the omni-bearing, wide-range and multilevel pattern of opening up has been basically formed. The great historic transition from the highly concentrated planned economic system to the vigorous socialist market economic system has significantly promoted the social productive forces, comprehensive national strength and people's living standard, created the brand-new conditions of political, economic, cultural and social development in

China and rendered the powerful driving force and institutional guarantee for the development of socialism with Chinese characteristics. The most important experience from successful Reform and Opening Up is the combination of the socialist system and the market economy as well as development of the market economy under socialist conditions.

II.   Contributions of practices on socialist market economy to scientific socialism

Based on laws and the trend of the development of human society, authors of classics of Marxism scientifically clarified the historical necessity for socialism to replace capitalism and revealed basic characteristics of the future society, which include social possession of means of production, planned regulation on social production, distribution on the basis of labor and demands, the elimination of antagonism between town and county and mental labor and physical labor and the free and all-around development of people, etc. These ideas of classics authors had pointed out the direction for socialist revolution and construction. However, these theories must be combined with practices and could only survive, last long and keep prosperous upon examination by practices and enrichment and development through practices. Development of the market economy under socialist conditions is an unprecedented great creative practice carried out by people under the leadership of the Party, as well as a historic contribution made by the Communist Party of China to Marxism and scientific socialism.

First, it has explored the connotation of socialism. Practices on construction and improvement of the socialist market economic system enabled us to change the traditional theories and models of socialism characterized by the rejection against commodity production and market mechanism and form the theories, road and system of the socialism with Chinese characteristics. To be specific, in terms of the structure of ownership, keep public ownership as the mainstay and allow diverse forms of ownership to develop side by side; regarding the distribution system, keep the labor-oriented distribution as the mainstay and allow diverse forms of distribution methods; in terms of economic operation, combine the fundamental role of market regulation with macro-control; for opening up, combine active participation in economic globalization and independence; and in terms of economic development, combine the pursuit of economic growth with people orientation. In conclusion, the practices of the Party leading people to develop socialist market economy since Reform and Opening Up first realize the combination of socialism and market economy in human history, endowed socialism with distinct characteristics of the times and Chinese characteristics, helped us profoundly change our understanding of socialism and enriched and developed connotation of socialism.

Second, it has realized innovation on the form to realize socialism. It has been the major subject in practices of scientific socialism that which system and mechanism should be applied to realize socialism. When promoting reform of the economic system, we have gradually established the new public ownership economic management system adapting to the market economy; optimized the layout and structure of the state-owned economy; made the shareholding system the major form to realize public ownership and strengthened the vigor, control and influence of public-owned economy; gradually established the system of distribution on the basis of labor adapting to requirements of the market economy; attached importance to economic efficiency; rationally widened the income gap, while preventing polarization between the poor and rich and maintained social equity to gradually realize common prosperity; established the socialist economic management system with Chinese characteristics including the overall planning, economic regulation, market supervision, social management, public service and state-owned asset management, formed the macro-control system based on the market mechanism; and gave full play to both plan and market. The establishment and constant improvement of the socialist market economic system have created the new vitality of the socialist system, helped us find the effective form to realize the basic socialist system in reality and fully unveiled the superiority of the socialist system.

Third, it has created the new form of the market economy. The market economy integrates generality and personality. The traditional market economy is combined with the capitalist system, which necessarily leads to profound defects and weaknesses such as blindness, spontaneity and hysteresis as well as economic crisis and polarization between the rich and the poor. The socialist market economy is combined with the basic socialist system and shows its unique social nature. Jiang Zemin pointed out, "The word 'socialist' cannot be missing. It is not unnecessary or superfluous; while, on the contrary, it is crucial that it points out the nature of our market economy".[2] The socialist market economy is a new form of the market economy featured with new characteristics and advantages compared to the traditional market economy. On the one hand, it gives full play to advantages of the market mechanism including sensitive information, high efficiency, efficient stimulus and flexible regulation, etc., and promotes the vigor of economic development, and, on the other hand, it gives full play to the advantages of socialism, which are beneficial to overcome defects and weaknesses of the capitalist market economy, and realize common prosperity of all society members and overall development of the society.

Chinese economic reform has acquired remarkable achievements. The most fundamental experience from the success lies in construction and improvement of the socialist economic system with Chinese characteristics. By developing the market economy under socialist conditions, it means, in addition to adhering to basic socialist system, it is necessary to give full play to the fundamental regulating role of the market mechanism in allocation of resources, mobilize enthusiasm of all parties, concern interests of all parties, make good use of resources from all parties and give full play to the superiority of the socialist system and advantages of the market economy. Facts speak louder than words. This socialist economic system with Chinese characteristics and the socialist market economic system provide great support for China to own relatively strong comprehensive national power and important international position, keep constant and stable development among the fierce international competition, withstand the test of major emergencies such as the radical social changes in the Soviet Union and Eastern Europe and East Asia Financial Crisis at the end of the 20th century and earthquake in 2008 and lead the world to realize economic stability and recovery in the global crisis. The socialist economic system with Chinese characteristics and the socialist market economic system have demonstrated the great superiority and vigor through practices.

III.   Essence of socialist market economy: dialectics of universality and particularity

The theoretical circle always has different understandings about the essence of the socialist market economy. Some scholars believe that the market economy is a method for resources allocation without social attributes, and the modern market economy may be advanced or backward but does not belong to "socialism" or "capitalism" only; some scholars believe that socialism means social equity and market economy means high efficiency, so the socialist market economy means adding market efficiency to social equity, and some believe that it is necessary to integrate to internationally universal economic laws if building the market economy, so it shall refer to the mode in advanced capitalist countries of the market economy and build the western-style market economic mode integrating privatization, liberalization and political pluralism. These opinions noted earlier are all one-sided, as they only see the generality but fail to discover the personality of the market economy and split the dialectical relationship between universality and particularity and the generality and personality, so they fail to correctly understand the essence of the market economy. The market economy is a common phenomenon that exists in different social systems, so it does not belong to "socialism" or "capitalism" only from this point of view; however, the market economy is always combined with certain social systems and considered a social and historical category, so it necessarily shows special social attributes and specific conditions. As pointed out by Karl Marx,

> Commodity production and commodity circulation exist in very different modes of production, despite their different scope and role. Therefore, though you understand the abstract scope of commodity circulation universal in these modes of production, you hardly understand any different characteristic of these modes of production or judge on these modes of production.[3]

The market economy, in reality, is the integration of universality and particularity and generality and personality. We shall not mix the market economy with capitalism and deny the generality of the market economy, or split the market economy with the social system and deny the personality of the market economy. In this sense, the theories of our Party are clear. When the Report of the 14th National Congress of CPC proposed the goal of economic reform in China as the socialist market economic system, it particularly emphasized, "The socialist market economic system is combined with basic socialist system". Deng Xiaoping pointed out that "What is the economic superiority of the socialist market economy? The answer is the Four Cardinal Principles".[4] The Report of the 17th National Congress of CPC regarded "combination of adherence to the basic socialist system and development of market economy" as an important historical experience from the success of Reform and Opening Up in China. Xi Jinping stressed on adhering to the direction of socialist market economic reform and adhering to dialectics and the doctrine affirming two aspects, continuing to put great effort on the combination of the basic socialist system and the market economy, and giving full play to advantages of both.

The socialist market economy is integrated with the basic socialist system. The integration, on the one hand, gives full play to advantages of the advantages of the market mechanism including the sensitive information, high efficiency, efficient stimulus and flexible regulation, etc., and promotes the vigor of economic development, and, on the other hand, gives full play to advantages of the socialist economy such as public ownership of means of production, distribution on the basis of labor, planned regulations, overall arrangement, independence, unity and mutual aid, which overcomes the inherent weaknesses of capitalist market economy of blindness, spontaneity and hysteresis and profound defects such as economic crisis and polarization between the rich and the poor. In this way, the socialist market economy has theoretically and practically surpassed the current dogma of the capitalist market economy with private ownership as the basis, significantly promoted development of social productive forces, rendered strong driving force and institutional guarantee for the development of socialism with Chinese characteristics and explored the unprecedented broad way for the development of scientific socialism and progress of human civilization. This is the fundamental reason for unswervingly adhering to the economic reform direction of the socialist market economy when deepening the reform of economic system.

IV. Socialist market economy developing the strength and discarding the dross of the capitalist market economy

What are the advantages of the socialist market economy compared to the capitalist market economy? To answer this question, the defects of the capitalist market economy shall be first clarified. As is known to all, the market economy is exposed to certain defects or disadvantages. However, due to influence of western mainstream economics, people's understanding of defects of the market economy has been significantly restrained. First, people often consider this question from the micro-view instead of the macro-view and believe that the defect of the market lies in the market failure – i.e. the monopoly, externality, public goods and information asymmetry, which restrains the role of the market. Second, people only underside this question from the universality but not from the particularity of the market economy and mix the market economies under different social systems. The two restraints severely impede people from scientifically understanding the essence of the market economy and its development laws.

The commodity economy has been existing for thousands of years, but had been only subject to small scale and scope before capitalism and was merely small commodity production or simple commodity economy. Along with the development of productive forces, particularly after the human society entered the capitalist society, commodity economy has ushered in significant development based on the development of socialization of production and labor employment of capitalism. Since then, the commodity economy has become the universal dominant social and economic form, the capitalist market economy or modern market economy.

The combination of capitalism and the market economy has endowed the market economy with unprecedented great vigor and creativity, meanwhile also brought about unprecedented product defects and damages to the market economy. As elaborated by Karl Marx, "The modern bourgeois society that once created such huge means of production and exchange with magic is now like a magician that can no longer control the devil he summoned".[5]

What are the profound defects of the capitalist market economy?

(1) Antagonism between labor and capital: Since the salary is inversely proportional to profit, upon certain newly created value, the capitalist often lower down the worker's salary and sacrifice the worker's interests to realize the maximum profits.

(2) Relative overpopulation or unemployment: The development of productive forces, improvement of organic composition of capital and relatively decreasing demand by capital on labor lead to severe unemployment, making the relative status of worker further deteriorated.

(3) Polarization between the poor and rich: Along with constant accumulation of capitals and deterioration of relative status of workers, the wealth is concentratedly owned by a small number of people, and the gap between the workers and bourgeois is constantly expanding.

(4) Overproduction crisis: The increasing conflict between the trend of unlimited expansion of the capitalist production and the relatively decreasing payment ability of workers necessarily leads to the economic crisis of overproduction.

(5) Blindness of development: The capitalist economic development has no overall plan or organization, while the balance between the social production and demands is spontaneously and compulsorily realized through constant economic fluctuation and turmoil, even the huge waste and damage of productive forces.

(6) Economic virtualization: The financial capital acquires the dominant position compared to all other forms of capitals along with the development of capitalism, and the fierce expansion of the virtual capitals and financial departments relative to the real economy leads to frequent financial crisis and severe financial speculation.

(7) Fierce ecological crisis: Endless pursuit of profits and no organization of social production necessarily result in global difficulties in population, resources, environment and ecology, exert increasing threats to environmental and ecological balance and damage the normal conditions for social reproduction.

(8)   Distortion of world market: On the one hand, the sovereign currency without value support such as USD plays the part of international currency, which damages the basic laws of commodity economy of exchange of equal values, and, on the other hand, international flow of labor forces is subject to strict control along with liberalization of trade and investment. Therefore, the market economy is incomplete and distorted worldwide.

The aforementioned defects of the capitalist market economy have been seldom mentioned in general textbooks on western economics. This is because western economics has no concept of capitalism. The market economy in western economics is the abstract and general market economy without any social or historic condition, the core idea of which refers to different behaviors carried out by rational people who pursue the maximum interests of their own to realize market balance. Obviously, this kind of economics can hardly give scientific explanation of internal laws, basic conflicts and historic trends of the capitalist market economy, or truly understand the fundamental defects of the modern market economy. It cannot find out the effective method to solve problems when these severe defects are exposed.

From the 18th century, when the production mode of capitalism emerged to the 1930s and the 1940s, the government had played the role as the "night watch" of the society and "outsider" of the market economy in the capitalist society and pursued laissez-faire. Encountered with the profound defects of the capitalist market economy after the 1929–1933 Great Depression, particularly after the World War II, the capitalist state, as the general representative of bourgeois, had to exert direct and indirect intervention on the economy, to guarantee economic stability and constant development and maintain the overall interests of capitalists. The laissez-faire policy was replaced by state interventionism, including building the state-owned economy, investing on basic industries, regulating on total social demands, creating the social welfare and security system, purchasing commodities and labors by the government and conducting market control, etc. These measures, adapted to the requirements of the development of productive forces to a certain extent, relieved the defects of the capitalist market economy and brought about the golden period of rapid growth in the 1950s and the 1960s. However, the defects of the market economy had not been eliminated in this way but had been increasingly intensified.

Since the 1970s, due to the "stagflation" crisis of co-existence of unemployment and inflation, the state interventionism was violently criticized, while the neoliberal policies with privatization, liberalization and minimum state intervention as the core have acquired the dominant position. Along with the global rapid expansion of the capitalist market economy, its internal conflicts and profound defects are also rapidly rising. As demonstrated by increasingly severe unemployment, intensified polarization, frequent financial and economic crisis, expropriation of the whole world by international monopoly capital, particularly the unprecedented disaster incurred by the rapid transition to capitalism in the

Soviet Union and Eastern Europe and the worldwide financial crisis that started in America in 2008, spread over the whole world and is still developing; the greater the development of the capitalist relation of production achieves, the sharper its internal conflict is and the more serious the crisis is. The real restraint on capitalist production is capital itself. Though the capitalist production always tries to overcome its inherent restraints, the measures it applies to overcome the restraints only make these restraints show up again on a larger scale,[6] thus leading to breakout of conflict and crisis in a wider range and broader area. This is the historic logic and dialectics.

Why does the state intervention fail to eliminate defects of the capitalist market economy? This is because the intervention by the capitalist government on the economy is always facing a fundamental conflict due to private ownership – i.e., the too weak state intervention can hardly solve the severe issues such as unemployment, economic crisis and polarization between the rich and poor inherent in capitalist market economy – and the too strong state intervention would damage the sacred and inviolable principle of private ownership and inhibit the vigor of the market economy.

Superficially, liberal economics and Keynesian economics have opposite opinions on the relationship between government and market, but their ways of thinking are consistent with each other. First, both of them build the theoretical system based on the assumption of the market economy of private ownership is the most efficient and both theories regard maintaining the capitalist system as their duties of economics. Second, their understanding on the relationship between the market and government adopts the metaphysical way of thinking and both consider the relation between the government and market as duality, and their difference lies in the proportion of the government and market and both do not concern whether the capitalist system itself shall be replaced by the socialist system. Therefore, both theories essentially comply with the capitalist ideology and thus both cannot fundamentally solve basic conflicts of capitalism.

As Karl Marx pointed out at an earlier time, "The sticking point of the bourgeois society lies in no conscious regulation on production since the beginning". Any conscious social supervision and adjustment during social production is regarded as infringement upon the capitalists' property right, freedom and "originality" of self-determination. The mingled market failure and government failure constitute an inevitable result of the development of basic capitalist conflicts, as well as the fundamental cause why the capitalist market economy cannot realize the constant and rapid development. As proved by facts, various measures applied by the capitalist countries to solve the crises only make these crises show up again on a larger scale. The capitalist market economy based on private ownership cannot realize the real and effective government intervention. Only by combining the socialist system and market economy, it can give full play to advantages of both the market economy and the socialist system, fundamentally overcome the profound defects of the capitalist market economy and explore the broader way for the development of social productive forces and human civilization progress.

V.   Institutional advantages of socialist market economy

The socialist market economy develops the strength and discards the dross of the capitalist market economy. It reflects the universal principle of the market economy and basic characteristics of the socialist system, gives consideration to both efficiency and equality and gives full play to the superiority of the socialist system and the advantages of the market economy. In this sense, the socialist market economy owns new characteristics and new advantages that surpass the capitalist market economy.

(1)   Development goal

In terms of development goal, the socialist market economy follows the goal of realization of all-around development of people and achievement of prosperity for all social members. The basic law of the capitalist economy is the law of residential value. Despite the great development of productive forces, the law also leads to class antagonism, polarization between the rich and poor, economic crisis, anarchic state of social production and other severe defects. In the socialist society, along with the establishment of public ownership of means of production and the elimination of class antagonism, all social members become the co-owners of means of production and form the economic relation of mutual aid and cooperation. The goal of production is no longer a small number of people exploiting most people, but to satisfy materials demanded by social members, which creates objective conditions for realization of all-around development of people and achievement of prosperity for all social members as well as the elimination of severe defects of the capitalist market economy.

Without any doubt, as diverse forms of ownership exist in the socialist market economy, particularly the private ownership, and state-owned enterprises are independent commodity producers, from the micro-economic perspective, both private enterprises and public-owned enterprises pursue maximum profits. Therefore, some laws of the capitalist market economy also play a part to certain scope and degree such as the law of residual value and capital accumulation, so some defects of the capitalist market economy such as the polarization between the poor and rich and economic crisis may also emerge to a certain scope and degree. However, from the perspective of the whole society, due to public ownership and distribution on the basis of labor as the mainstay and the macro-control by the socialist country, the goal of production development or resources allocation is no longer to pursue maximum profits, but to satisfy material and cultural demands of people to the maximum extent and to realize the all-around development of people and achieve common prosperity of the whole society – i.e. people-oriented development.

In order to realize the people-oriented development under the socialist market economy, it shall not rely on traditional planned economy or the free market economy but depend on a series of specific and efficient systems and mechanism, including developing people's democracy, maintaining social equality and justice and guaranteeing people's rights on equal participation and equal development;

adhering to improving basic economic system; safeguarding people's common interests; promoting healthy development of non-public economies and making it the builder of the undertakings of socialism with Chinese characteristics; adjusting the structure of income distribution, maintaining social equality and justice, solving the issue of income gap and spreading the development achievements to all people in a fairer way; and building and improving the people's livelihood security system and trying to guarantee education, labor remuneration, medical care, elderly care and housing of people. These systems and mechanisms help realize the socialist production goal under the socialist market economy.

(2) Ownership structure

In terms of ownership structure, the socialist market economy is built on the basis of keeping public ownership as the mainstay of the economy and allowing diverse forms of ownership to develop side by side. The socialist market economy regards public ownership as the basis, combines the public ownership and market economy, contains the blindness, spontaneity and hysteresis of the market economy from the institutional perspective and explores broader prospects for the development of the market economy. By improving the mechanism of flexible and rational flow of state-owned capitals, optimizing the structure and layout of state-owned economies and strengthening the control, influence and competitiveness of state-owned economies, it will give better play to the leading role of state-owned economies in the national economy and therefore enhance the stability and coordination of the market economic operation and avoid great fluctuation. By building the rational enterprise system and harmonious socialist labor relation for public-owned enterprises and giving considerations to interests of the state, collective, individual and all parties, it improves the harmony of the market economy. By providing public commodities, investing in infrastructure, guaranteeing national economy and people's livelihood and combining economic development with the social development goal, it improves the benefits of the market economy and realizes the organic unity of efficiency and equality.

The characteristics and advantages of the socialist market economy also derive from the common development of diverse forms of ownership. By building and improving the modern enterprise system, the public-owned enterprises participate in the market competition equally as the market subject, which is beneficial to promote vigor and competitiveness of the public economy, give play to the superiority of the socialist system and guide, promote and drive development of non-public economy. Development of the non-public economy adapts to the requirements of the development of productive forces at the current stage in China, benefits urban and rural economic prosperity, increases fiscal income, expands social employment, improves people's living standards, optimizes economic structure and promotes vigor of the market economy. It shall be emphasized that other than a small number of enterprises wholly invested and operated by the government, most public-owned enterprises have diversified subjects of investment. The share-holding system has become a major form to realize the public ownership, while the mixed-ownership economy with state-owned capitals, collective capitals and non-public capitals has come into being. Under socialist market economy, diverse forms of ownership compete with each other, show their advantages and realize common development, which provides powerful and constant driving force for economic development in China.

As demonstrated by practices of the socialist market economy, combination of the public ownership and market economy gives full play to the fundamental role of the market mechanism in allocation of resources, renders new driving force and platform for the development of the market economy and provides powerful guarantee for overall economic and social progress and all-around development of people.

(3)   Distribution system

In terms of the distribution system, the socialist market economy keeps the labor-oriented distribution as the mainstay and allows diverse forms of distribution methods. Distribution on the basis of labor is the major principle for distribution in the socialist market economy. Application of the distribution principle helps mobilize the initiative and creativity of the vast number of workers and creates conditions for the elimination of exploitation and polarization and the ultimate achievement of prosperity for all. The distribution on the basis of labor directly links the labor of each worker to the remuneration, so each work concerns about the labor results due to the material interests. Emphasis on more work more pay and realization of labor equality and remuneration equality helps realize equality and justice of social distribution. As pointed out by Deng Xiaoping, "The too large gap between the rich and poor will not emerge if we adhere to socialism and the principle of distribution on the basis of labor".

In the socialist market economy, by keeping the labor-oriented distribution as the mainstay and allowing diverse forms of distribution methods, it allows the distribution based on contributions by various production factors such as capital, knowledge, technology, information, management, land and other natural resources, which is beneficial to mobilize economic entities; vitalize all labor, knowledge, technology, management and capital; enable the smooth and abundant flow of all sources that create the social wealth; and make full and efficient use of various resources. Determined by the current ownership structure in China, the co-existence of diverse forms of distribution methods adapts to the development level and development requirements of productive forces at the primary stage of socialism and is favorable to facilitate the development of productive forces.

To adhere to the distribution system of keeping the labor-oriented distribution as the mainstay and allowing diverse forms of distribution methods, it is necessary to overcome issues such as widening gap and imbalance in income distribution. Causes for emergence of these issues in income distribution in current China are complicated and diversified. We shall see that based on the labor-oriented distribution, the certain gap between the income level and living standard of workers is inevitable due to the actual difference in labor capability of workers and number of people and composition of their family. Meanwhile, the distribution system of keeping the labor-oriented distribution as the mainstay and allowing diverse forms of distribution methods shall be further improved in practices of the socialist market economy. Divorce of the labor and income, low labor income, gray income and illegal income, etc., affect the equality of distribution to a certain degree and damage the initiative and creativity of workers. Therefore, it is necessary to gradually increase the proportion of residents' income in the national income and the proportion of labor remuneration in primary distribution, thus to popularize the code of conduct of acquiring wealth through hard work, improve the pricing mechanism decided by the market supply, demand mechanism and competition mechanism and make remuneration from various production factors meet their contributions. Based on constant development of production, we shall generally improve people's income standard, avoid the polarization, lead the road of common prosperity and share the results of reform and development with all people.

(4) Regulation method

In terms of the method for economic regulation, the socialist market economy makes full use of two regulation methods, namely, control and market. Transition from laissez-faire to state intervention is common in development of the capitalist market economy. State intervention emerged because the capitalist market economy had been exposed to serious economic and social issues such as market failure, economic crisis and polarization between the poor and rich along with development of production socialization and expansion of the market economy scale, which went against stability and development of capitalism. However, due to fundamental institutional causes, state intervention in the capitalist market economy can only release these issues to a certain degree but cannot fundamentally solve these issues. It could be seen that along with the implementation of neoliberalism centering on privatization and liberalization after the 1980s, the defects and disadvantages of the capitalist market economy have been deteriorated instead of having been released. All measures applied by the capitalist country to solve the crises only make these crises show up again on a larger scale. As proved by facts, the capitalist market economy based on private ownership cannot carry out truly efficient state intervention.

Showing essential differences with the state intervention in the capitalist market economy, the state control of the socialist market economy not only emphasizes the regulation role of the market but also stresses the guiding role of state control; it not only reflects general characteristics of the modern market economy but also reveals unique advantages of the socialist system, and it not only focuses on effective market but also focuses on capable government. First, the subject of the state control is not only the one who formulates market regulations and regulates the macro-economy but also the general representative of the means of production owned by the whole people and social public interests, so it can concentrate more resources to regulate on and control economic operation. Second, the goal of state control is not only limited to maintaining the market order and creating macro-conditions for stable operation of the market mechanism but also emphasizes on establishing the economic development strategy that complies with fundamental interests of the overwhelming majority of the people and guiding the national economy to develop along the correct direction. Third, the measures for state control are not only limited to the fiscal policies and monetary policies but also combine demands on economic and social development and the fiscal and material resources of the society and underline the role of overall plan, coordination, market supervision, state-owned assets management and industry policies, etc. We should also know that the goal of common prosperity cannot be realized merely relying on the strength of the market, which also requires the government controlling the wealth distribution, maintaining the social equality and justice to the great extent and promoting social harmony. Fourth, the pattern of state control is not limited to the short-term control of the total volume, but perfect integrates the current and long-term control, total volume and structure control, supply and demand control and central and local control, as well as the market adjustment and state control, to strongly show the unique advantages of macro-control in socialist market economy.

(5)   Pattern of opening up

Regarding the pattern of opening up, socialist market economy actively participates in economic globalization and adheres to the opening-up policy of mutual benefits and win-win. Economic globalization is the objective requirement and inevitable outcome of production socialization and the development of the market economy. Economic globalization constantly improves the degree of production socialization, promotes the worldwide flow of commodities, labors, capitals and technologies, enable more rational allocation of production factors and vigorously promote the development of productive forces of human society. However, we shall also see that economic globalization is a double-edged sword. The current economic globalization is the globalization of the capitalist production relations guided by western developed countries and inevitably shows the features of capitalism and leads to a series of new conflicts, such as worldwide polarization, over-development and damage of the global ecological system, power concentrated in a small number of economic units free from any supervision or control, global economic chaos, constant financial crisis and deeper dependence of developing countries on developed countries.

Socialist market economy seeks for constant development by actively participating in economic globalization, adheres to both opening up and independence and attempts to achieve cooperation and win-win to benefit people worldwide. First, the socialist market economy is an open economy that is dedicated to building an omni-bearing, multilevel and wide-range pattern of opening up, makes full use of domestic and international markets and resources, combines "going out" and "bringing in" and constantly develops itself through constant expansion of opening up. Second, the socialist market economy is the major stable strength of worldwide market economy, insists on placing the domestic market as the basis and focus, promotes economic and social development through independent strength and reform and innovation, attaches importance to control over the key industry and sector, lowers the impact and damage incurred by worldwide economic fluctuation and does not transfer issues and conflicts to other countries. Finally, the socialist market economy adheres to the opening-up strategy of mutual benefits and win-win, emphasizes on the consistency between its own interests and common interests of humanity, attempts to realize favorable interaction with development of other countries while pursuing development itself and promotes the common development of all countries worldwide. As demonstrated by practices, the socialist market economy follows the development trend of economic globalization, helps the constant development of the Chinese economy, builds increasingly closer economic connection with all countries and regions and makes significant contributions to the economic development of the world.

However, we shall also see that by now, the economic globalization is developing under guidance by developed capitalist countries and inevitably shows features of the capitalist market economy. Therefore, development of economic globalization is necessarily accompanied by deepening and expansion of basic capitalist conflicts in the world range. It intensifies the imbalance between the south-north development, leads to deeper independence of developing countries on developed countries and causes increasingly larger gap between the rich and poor all over the world; it increases uncertain factors to world economic development and results in constant turbulence of the world economy and aggravates overdevelopment and exploitation of global energies and resources and leads to deteriorated global energy crisis and ecological crisis, etc. In terms of economic globalization, the socialist market economy opposes current unfair and irrational phenomenon in the international economic order, attempts to establish the fair and rational new international economic order and promotes the development of economic globalization in a more balanced, inclusive and mutual-benefits direction.

(6) Economic democracy

In terms of democratic system, the socialist market economy is integrated with the socialist democracy. Compared to the slavery system and feudal system, capitalism has realized democratic politics, which is undoubtedly a great historic progress. However, democracy in the capitalist society is the democracy based on capital and money to a great extent, which derives from the capitalist private ownership and serves for the capitalist private ownership. According to the analysis of American scholar Charles Edward Lindblom, the polyarchy or multiparty politics in capitalist society provides an efficient institutional structure for the business community with privileges to control the government. The control is realized through several channels as follows:

Under any private ownership, a series of major decisions are under control of businessmen, who actually became a kind of public official and acquired the right to control public affairs;

For the sake of normal economic operation, public decisions of the government have to give in to the business community and satisfy their requirements, so the businessmen acquire the wide influence over public decisions of the government in this way.

Based on abundant funds, prepared organizational structure and special channels approaching the government, the business community enjoys the leading role in competition for the control power over polyarchy, etc.[7]

Therefore, American scholar Charles Edward Lindblom believes that the western multiparty politics is linked to the market system not because it is democratic, but because it is not democratic. If all previous and current polyarchies are dominated by the business community and property, the few people at the dominating position would like to underline its relation with the market mechanism as the cause. It means that the real democracy may not rely on the market mechanism. The current polyarchy, though it advocates freedom, is actually controlled by the business community and the property relation in a non-democratic way.[8]

The economic foundation determines the superstructure, and different economic relations require different state institutions and democratic structures. In the socialist system, the political democracy develops directly from the public ownership of means of production, which features special advantages compared to the capitalist democratic system.

First, the polyarchy of capitalism is the product of private market economy and the institutional structure for free exchange of private properties. The socialist democracy regards the public ownership as the main body, while the public ownership of means of production realize the equal relationship of workers to the occupation of the means of production and makes workers the owners of the society. In this way, people are conferred upon with the right to be the master and manage public means of production and social resources in a democratic way, and democracy becomes an inherent attribute of the socialist system.

Second, the multiparty system of capitalism turns the specific interests of ordinary citizens to the abstract interests of party and summarizes the democratic power of ordinary citizens as the voting right that is fulfilled once several years, but actually rejects these people's specific rights as the direct and real representatives of these interests and the right to exert influence on political decision making.[9] The socialist democracy requires guaranteeing people's right as the owner of the country, expands citizen's orderly political participation from all levels and all areas, develops democracy at the grassroots level and promotes consultative democracy.

Third, the multiparty competition system of the capitalist society creates the diversified political group, aggravates conflicts between all classes and ranks of the society, hinders realization of common interests and collective will and affects the efficiency of public decision-making. However, the political representative organization and political representatives generated based on the socialist public ownership directly come from social members, represent interests of all organizations, all classes and all aspects of the society, bear responsibilities for social members they represent and are subject to supervision by social members represented by them.

Therefore, democracy in the socialist system always integrates economy and politics together, and the economic democracy is an important part of the socialist democratic politics. As early as in the 1950s, Mao Zedong pointed out, "Workers' rights to manage the state, the troop, all enterprises and cultural education are actually their largest and most fundamental rights in the socialist system, which truly demonstrates the socialist democracy".[10] When elaborating the standards on democratic system, Xi Jinping regarded "whether all people could manage the state affairs and social affairs, economy and cultural undertakings according to laws, whether people could smoothly express their interest requirements, whether all aspects of the society can effectively participate in national political life and whether decisions of the state are scientific and democratic", etc., as the major principle. The Constitution of China emphasizes the democratic nature of state management and proposes, "The state-owned enterprises shall realize democratic management through employees' representative conference and other forms according to laws" and "the collective economy shall apply democratic management, select and dismiss any manager according to laws and decide on major issues related to operation and management". All these fully demonstrate the coherent connection between socialist economy and democracy.

Democracy also shows another special significance in the socialist market economy. The development of the market economy will necessarily widen the gap on wealth occupation and income distribution of people, aggravate the antagonism between labor and capital, lead to actual inequality on people's economic, political and social status, easily breed corruption of power-money trade, damage the equality and justice of the society, result in social differentiation and slit and erode and break down the socialist system. There is no socialism or socialist market economy if no democracy. During development of socialist market economy, it is necessary to promote democracy, improve the democratic system, perfect the democratic decision making, democratic management and democratic supervision, widely converge people's wisdom, inspire people's strength and create the situation where all people participate in, do their best and earn their sense of achievement, so that all people could enjoy the achievements of reform and development. In this way, it can fundamentally inhibit the spreading of bureaucracy and corruption, guarantee people's common interests and safeguard the healthy development of the socialist system.

In conclusion, the socialist market economy is a new form of economic system established on exploration by China, the biggest developing country in the world. It is different to the totally market-oriented economic system in America, the high-welfare and high-tax economic system in Europe and even the economic systems of other developing countries and emerging industrialized countries. As a great invention by contemporary China, the socialist market economy is an important enlightenment and experience for the large number of developing countries of the current world that aims to get rid of poverty and realize the development of the state to select the development road. Despite the short history, the socialist market economy has revealed its great superiority and powerful vigor. Along with constant development and improvement, the economic system will make great contributions to the development of human civilization.

VI.   Several theoretical propositions on market economy that needs reflection

Rich practices of the socialist market economy provide unusual experiences for the profound understanding of the essence and structure of the market economy, deepen our thinking about the market economy from many aspects and inspire us of reflections on many theoretical propositions and popular ideas on market economy.

(1) Is the market economy merely a way of resources allocation? It is a popular opinion to view the market economy as a method of allocation of scarce resources. This idea only focuses on the superficial process of the market but fails to unveil the profound social connotation and complicated inherent structure of the market economy. If the market economy is regarded as a way of resources allocation, it is considered from not only its material content but more importantly its social form. From the perspective of political economics, commodities are not materials, but a special economic relationship between people covered by the form of materials. Essentially, allocation of resources refers to allocation of resources among different people showing interest difference and even interest conflict, so the production relation of the whole society based on certain ownership and the superstructure based on the production relation constitute the social foundation for realization of the resources allocation. Superficially, market mechanism regards price as the core, so the major content of reform shall be controlling the currency and relaxing price controls. However, price is based on value, while value again reflects the relation of free exchange between economic entities with independent property right. Therefore, without reform of the ownership system, the price signal cannot fully play its role. Moreover, the fundamental reform of the ownership system requires the complete market of production factors, perfect legal system and relatively perfect social security system, as well as corresponding political-legal relation and ideology. Politically, the market economy demands independent and free individual identity, fully developed civil and commercial law system and apparent divorce between the government and market. Ideologically, development of the market economy is necessarily accompanied by increasing awareness of independence, freedom, competition, efficiency, material gains and contract and demands the corresponding cultural atmosphere. Finally, all these factors are based on development of social productive forces. Increasing growth of economic surplus, increasingly richer social demands, increasing improvement of people's capability, increasing wider range of division of labors and innovation of technologies and products promote the development of the market economy from the low level to the high level. Therefore, market economy is not only a way of resources allocation but also a special social form. Transition to the market economy not only involves transition of the way of resources allocation but also is a long-term, complicated and overall

process covering profound changes to economic, political and cultural aspects of the society.

(2) Is the market economy a neutral concept? Based on the idea that the market mechanism is a method of resources allocation, the market socialism theory made use of the analysis tool of neoclassical economics to build its initial theoretical mode – i.e. the Lange-Lerner-Taylor Mode (Lange Mode).[11] This mode assumed the market mechanism to be neutral without any system attribute and had exerted wide influence over the socialist economic theories and market-orientation reform. However, though the idea of the neutral nature broke with the anti-market tradition in the socialist economic theories, derived the market mechanism from the capitalist system and thus theoretically explored the road for integration of socialism and market economy, it was fundamentally unhistorical, ignored the special social attributes and historical nature of the market economy and could not build the scientific economic theory of socialist market. The commodity exchange and market mechanism is an ordinary economic phenomenon existing in many social forms and does not belong to a certain social system. In this sense, the mechanism is neutral since it does not belong to capitalism or socialism. However, it does not mean that the market mechanism is a technical tool that independently exists without special historical environment or overall social structure or that can be copied arbitrarily in different institutional environment. Practically, the market economy itself is a special economic relationship or institutional form. The nature, status and role of the market mechanism vary in different historical development stages and different institutional environment. From this perspective, the market mechanism is not completely neutral. The classical market economy is different from modern market economy, the market economy in developing countries is different from the market economy in developed countries, and the socialist market economy is different from the capitalist market economy. The marketization reform in China by now is based on the socialist Constitution and connected to the institutional reform, so the socialism and the market economy have formed a complicated relation of mutual influence, mutual penetration and mutual restriction. On the one hand, the transition to the market economy in China is conducted based on the socialist Constitution, which fundamentally determines the model and road of marketization of China and specifies the possibility frontier and basic restraints on marketization of China. You will never truly understand the essence and process of economic reform in China if you do not know this. On the other hand, the practical socialism is built on the basis of the market economy, while the generation of the market relation will conversely promote reform of the Constitution system and changes to the ownership, so socialism is given the new meaning. The essence and difficulty in economic transition of China lies in how to realize the transition of the socialist economic relation from the old system to the new system during marketization and combine socialism with the market economy.

(3) Is the market economy a free economy? According to economic liberalism, market economy is the code word for free economy, and the market mechanism independently adjusts and leads rational allocation of resources like an invisible hand that is free from the effect of politics and other social forces, etc. The theories of economic liberalism had once played a positive role in breaking restraints by the feudal system and promoting development of the market economy and productive forces. However, it became too ideological in contemporary times. As market economy emphasizes on personal interests, independent decision making and free competition, it can be regarded as a free economy in this sense. However, it contains a basic conflict right since the beginning – i.e., the conflict between private labor and social labor based on social division of labor. Division of labor, on the one hand, separates different producers and make them free and independent commodity producers, and, on the other hand, creates the mutual dependence between them, as everyone can only survive relying on others. This basic conflict of the market economy generates the requirements of economic freedom but meanwhile gives rise to various factors that deny the free market: as some enterprises are organized and the whole social production has no government control, the free market will inevitably lead to the imbalance of the macro-economy and the macro-control becomes necessary; since the production shows the trend of unlimited expansion but the market demand is relatively small due to the antagonism between labor and capital within the distribution relation, it is necessary for the state to regulate on the income distribution and establish the social welfare system; as the relationship between people has been completely materialized in the market economy, when individuals gain greater freedom, their mutual dependence and conflicts are increasingly intensified, so the social cooperation and social regulation widely develop outside the market competition; the equality in the form of exchange process conceals the inequality in facts and free competition will definitely lead to polarization and the concentrated wealth and monopoly of power against the marginalized vulnerable group, which requires economic democracy and equality; successful market transaction demands the ownership system and market order adapting to the market relation, and the establishment and improvement of the ownership system and market order are only the product of political activities of human. Finally, the fact is inconsistent with what economic liberals believe that when everyone pursues personal private interests, they would attain the collectivity of private interests – i.e., common interests. "The other conclusion can be drawn from the abstract idea: everyone is hindering others realizing their interests. The war of everyone opposing everyone only results in general negation instead of general recognition".[12] Consequentially, the pure free market economy is unsustainable. The market mechanism must be guaranteed by non-market factors and freedom must be restrained, so we can see the historical trend for existence and the development of the market economy from the transition from the free

market economy to the market economy under regulation, emergence of state interventionism, widely application of macro-policies, expansion of the scope of public choices and permeation of various non-market organizations and non-market factors into the process of market.

(4) Is the market economy a product of spontaneous order? Can the market economy be planed and designed? Can the process of marketization be planned and controlled? Two opposite opinions exist on this issue. According to the evolution doctrine, the generation and development of the market economy follows spontaneous evolution, while this process is unknowable, uncontrollable and uncertain. Constructivism holds the exactly opposite opinion and believes that the process of institutional transition is knowable, controllable and certain and therefore can be artificially constructed. Both ideas are rational but meanwhile one-sided. Practically, the market economy is both the product of spontaneous order and the result of social construction. On the one hand, the market economy is essentially spontaneous, a social form that adjusts division of labor and allocation of resources, with spontaneous division of labor and market exchange as the basis, the private interests and competition as the driving force and the supply and demand and price as the mechanism. Therefore, its generation and evolution is largely spontaneous and uncertain, and people cannot make accurate design of this process and completely follow the pre-designed blueprint in implementation. The transition to the market economy incorporates many trials. During Reform and Opening Up of China, the reform from bottom to top, step-by-step progress, dual-track transition and experiments before spreading, etc., that have been applied have reflected the essence of transition of institutional change. As the market economy is exposed to historical evolution, the market economy as the reform goal is not fixed. From the theory of "leading role of the planned economy and the supplementary role of market regulation" in the 12th National Congress of CPC, the theory of planned commodity economy in the 3rd Plenary Session of the 12th Central Committee of the Party, the economic operating mode of "government regulating on market and market guiding enterprises" in the 13th National Congress to the socialist market economy put forward in the 14th National Congress, people's understanding about the reform goal has been developing and deepening, which also shows the feature of evolution. However, it shall be also noticed that the evolution doctrine believes that the process of social evolution is only the product of unconscious acts of people, is only exposed to spontaneous evolution and cannot be artificially constructed, which does not comply with facts. On the contrary, any legal social rules are formulated and enforced by the government and are all "public products" that could be consciously designed and enforced. Particularly, under the framework of the socialist constitutional system, the process of economic reform needs to be conducted under more organizational control compared to other societies. In the process of economic reform in China, it is the government that constructs and promotes generation and development of reform theories, presentation and

adjustment of the reform goal, design and selection of the reform proposal, formulation and implementation of reform policies, revision to the constitutional system, construction of market rules and release of major reform measures, etc. The human society is subject to both evolution and construction, and is spontaneous and meanwhile selective. It is a basic subject of economic transition that how to well handle the relation between spontaneous order and social rationality.

(5) Is the market economy the exchange economy or contract economy? Market economy is a kind of economic form based on commodity exchange, while all economic relations in market economy are first presented as the equal contract relation between independent commodity producers. Therefore, market economy was generally known as the contract economy. However, it is superficial to conclude the market economy as the contract economy, because it fails to reflect the deep structure of the market economy. Why did the market emerge? What decides the development of market? Why does the same market economy show such great differences in different countries and different development stages? To answer these questions, it shall go deep from the superficial market transactions to the inside of production. This is because production determines exchange, the division of labor constitutes the foundation of the market economy, and the depth, range and method of exchange are decided by the development level and structure of labor division and production.[13] The essence of the exchange relation is decided by production relations, while the content of the contract relation is given by the content of production relations. For example, the contract on purchasing and sale of labor is different from the contract on exchange of material products, and the contract on commodity exchange is different from the contract on capital exchange, etc. In this way, generation and development of the market economy greatly depends on transition of the production structure, particularly the conditions of labor division and ownership. Between them, the ownership structure directly determines development of the market economy, while the development of productive force and labor division plays the fundamental role. The difference between market economies of different types, particularly between the developed market economy and underdeveloped market economy, fundamentally result from different development level of productive forces as well as different development level of labor division and specialization. The same market system shows significant differences and attains different economic performance in developed countries and developing countries. The modern market economy cannot be rapidly built purely relying on release of control on price, cancellation of government control or simulation of the constitutional system of developed capitalist countries without advanced productivity and highly developed labor division. As a developing country in the process of transition, the market development and role of the market mechanism in China is subject to both restraints of social systems and the

development level of productive forces. Economic development in current China is still in the middle stage of industrialization. Due to backward productive forces, the development of the market economy is exposed to restrictive factors such as rough labor division, simple structure, inhibited information flow, inconvenient traffic, poor infrastructure, large gap between the urban and rural area, too low industrialization, backward science and culture, insufficient resources and capitals and weak competitive power in foreign countries, so the depth, scope and completeness of market development have been greatly restricted. It decides that the market economy formed in the current stage of China is only a low-level imperfect market economy.

(6) Is the Reform directing socialist market economy equal to the Reform directing marketization? A popular opinion since Reform and Opening Up believes that the so-called economic system reform is actually the marketization reform, and reform is actually marketization. This point of view made sense at the early stage of the Reform compared to the traditional planned economic system. However, in the strict sense, this is unscientific and inaccurate, because marketization is not an isolated phenomenon but is related to certain social system. As the reform goal, the socialist market economy consists of two aspects, first, giving full play to the fundamental regulating role of market mechanism in allocation of resources, and second, adhering to improving the basic economic system of socialism. To give play to the decisive role of the market mechanism, it requires establishing the enterprise system of independent operation, pricing mechanism based on market and perfect market system, full market competition, while the Reform in these areas can be shortly called the marketization reform. To improve the basic economic system of socialism, it requires establishing the basic economic system that keeps public ownership as the mainstay of the economy and allows diverse forms of ownership to develop side by side as well as the distribution system that keeps the labor-oriented distribution as the mainstay and allows diverse forms of distribution methods, gives play to the macro-control role of the socialist state, guarantees equality and justice of society and realizes common prosperity of social members. The Reform in these areas cannot be concluded as the marketization reform, and even is contrary to marketization reform, which corrects, regulates on and exceeds the limitations and weaknesses of the market economy and reflects the superiority of socialism. In socialist market economy, it is the basic requirement of deepening reform to give full play to the market mechanism and realize marketization of resources, but it also requires improving the basic economic system and distribution system, realizing common prosperity and guaranteeing equality and justice to deepen reform. Only organic combination of these two aspects can completely and accurately reflect the essence of socialist market economy and requirements of the socialist market economy reform.

VII.   Better integration of socialism and market economy

Since the 3rd Plenary Session of the 18th Central Committee of CPC, the economic system reform in China has ushered in a new stage when diverse reform measures are in process. The key to success of the new round of reform lies in adhering to the correct direction, promoting reform in the correct path, unswervingly adhering to the reform direction of the socialist market economy and realizing the self-improvement and development of the socialist system.

What are the major issues encountered when deepening the economic system reform? The common answer to this question may be the residue of the old planned economy, or halfway marketization reform, over control by the government on micro-economic activities and the market not given full play to – for example, the too wide range of administrative approval, too concentrated power, prices of some important resources and production factors that have not been rationalized, serious administrative tendency in operation and management of state-owned enterprises and institutions, lack of standardization and no universal rules in market order, departmental and regional protectionism and division of the urban and rural system, etc. Therefore, the Reform on relevant areas must be carried out to give full play to the decisive role of the market, including significantly reducing the government's direct allocation of resources, facilitating the improvement of the modern market system and further promoting market vigor. This answer is undoubtedly correct, and this is one major direction of current economic system reform in China.

However, we shall know that this is only one aspect of the question. Some other issues cannot be simply attributed to the residue of the old planned economy or halfway marketization reform, such as overcapacity, unemployment, gap between the rich and poor, economic fluctuation, power-money trade, environmental pollution, food and drug safety, construction of people's livelihood and insufficient social security. These issues are inherent defects of the market economy to a great extent and cannot even be avoided in the developed capitalist market economy. It is absolutely useless if trying to solve inherent defects of marketization by so-called complete marketization. The fundamental approach to overcome these defects is to play the advantages of socialism and increase the attribute of socialism of the market economy.

We shall realize that the economic foundation of China has been exposed to fundamental changes through over three decades of in-depth reform. The non-public economies have occupied half of the economic life, the capitalist factor has attained considerable development, and capitals are exerting the profound effect on class relations, political structure and ideology of China. Such a change and economic, political and cultural penetration by western hostile forces severely challenge the leadership of the Communist Party of China and the socialist system, making the task to control the market economy especially the capitals extremely complicated and difficult. We shall see both the compatibility and conflict between socialism and market economy, and between socialism and private economy. The socialist system features its own particular prescriptions, such as the elimination of exploitation and polarization, guarantee of equality and justice, the ultimate achievement of prosperity for all, planned development and workers in power. To realize these prescriptions, it is necessary to rely on the market but shall never completely rely on the market mechanism. By purely depending on the spontaneous market economy, it cannot realize the goal of socialism but will lead to the wrong way of capitalism. Ignoring this, it may result in major subversive historical changes. The vital question is which, between socialism and market economy, between the Communist Party and the state led by the Party and capital, is the controller and master. This is the most fundamental challenge and the most acute problem for deepening reform of the economic system.

From this point of view, we need a correct understanding of the decisive role of the market. It shall be emphasized that under socialist conditions, a prerequisite must be followed to give play to the decisive role of the market, which is consolidating and promoting the leadership of the Party, the active role of the government and the basic social system. If not observing the prerequisite, the decisive role of the market would be necessarily transferred to the decisive role of capitals, making capitals the decisive power in social economy, politics and culture. At that time, the political power and social system would be changed, socialism would be replaced by capitalism, antagonism between labor and capital would be intensified, the wealth distribution would be polarized and private capitals particularly large capitals would emerge, which would lead to the generation of financial oligarchy, break social stability, result in social chaos, shake the foundation of socialist undertakings with Chinese characteristics and, finally, severely inhibit healthy development of productive forces. This is the objective law not subject to the subjective will of people that historical materialism tells us.

Therefore, in order to adhere to the reform direction of socialist market economy, on the one hand, it is required to handle the relation between government and market well, enable the market to play the decisive role in allocation of resources, help the government play a better party and improve efficiency of allocation of resources, and, on the other hand, it is required to adhere to and improve the basic socialist system and give full play to the superiority of the socialist system. More market, more socialism and better integration of socialism and market economy make up the correct direction and strategic selection to comprehensively deepen reform.

The current problem is that how to truly reflect and realize the correct direction and strategic selection in practices of comprehensively deepening reform, instead of regarding it as merely a slogan. This is the most important and fundamental issue of current economic system reform deepening that is most easily ignored. Where shall we start to realize more socialism among numerous mature experiences and practices on playing the role of the market and numerous policies and measures for choice? Problems and solutions emerge at the same time, which mainly include the following. First, consolidate and promote the public-owned economy including the state-owned economies and rural collective economies, never engage itself in privatization and meanwhile constantly improve the mechanism of public-owned economies to help it better combine with the market economy and better satisfy interests of all people. Second, care-fully implement the principle of labor-oriented distribution, encourage labor and creation, practically solve the issue on too large gap of wealth and income distribution, strengthen regulation on property income, gradually start to collect the property tax, legacy tax, gift tax, housing tax and luxury consumption tax, increase the tax rate of resources tax and apply it as the wealth source to improve the social security, public welfare and life of low-income earners, significantly increase the income of workers and head to the direction of common prosperity. Third, adhere to and improve leadership of the Party; enhance the capability to govern the state; give better play to the government; promote the schedule and efficiency of macro-control; try to overcome the blindness, spontaneity and hysteresis, as well as serious defects of the market economy including oligop-oly, economic crisis, polarization, money politics and ecological damages, etc.; and, constantly, promote the capability to control the socialist market economy. Fourth, adhere to our independence, initiative and self-reliance, regard our own strength as the standing point, improve the ability of independent innovation, firmly safeguard state sovereignty and security in opening up, maintain the fair and rational international order and pursue common interests of all people around the world. Fifth, ensure the well-being of the people and improve their lives, try to guarantee education, labor remuneration, medical care, elderly care and housing of people and constantly improve the living standards and well-being of people. Sixth, vigorously promote economic democracy, lead the mass line, guarantee people's status as the master and right in management in economic activities at the enterprise, government and other levels and try to overcome bureaucracy and corruption. Seventh, adhere to and improve the socialist political system and core value system, and consolidate and strengthen the superstructure of socialism.

Ultimately, the masses are the creators of history. Only reform for people and reform relying on people can make reform the real common undertakings of all people, broaden the road of socialism with Chinese characteristics, realize the great rejuvenation of the Chinese nation and make greater contributions to the progress of humanity.

Notes

1 Deng Xiaoping, *Talking Points in Wuchang, Shenzhen, Zhuhai and Shanghai etc.*, 1992, Vol. 3 of *Selected Works of Deng Xiaoping*, People's Publishing House, Edition 1994, Page 373.
2 Jiang Zemin, *On Socialist Market Economy*, CPC Archives Publishing House, Edition 2006, Page 202–203.
3 Karl Marx, *Capital*, People's Publishing House, Edition 2004, Page 133.
4 CPC Central Committee Archives Research Office, *Chronicle of Deng Xiaoping (1975–1997)*, Vol. 2, CPC Archives Publishing House, Edition 2004, Page 1363.
5 *Selected Works of Marx and Engels*, Vol. 1, People's Publishing House, Edition 2012, Page 406.
6 Karl Marx, *Capital*, Vol. 3, People's Publishing House, Edition 2004, Page 278.
7 See the earlier analysis in relevant part in *Politics and Markets* by Charles Edward Lindblom, Shanghai Joint Publishing Press, Edition 1992.

8 Charles Edward Lindblom, *Politics and Markets*, Shanghai Joint Publishing Press, Edition 1993, Page 245.

9 See the analysis of this question in *Democracy and Socialism* by Edvard Kardelj, People's Publishing House, Edition 1981.

10 CPC Central Committee Archives Research Office, *Chronicle of Mao Zedong 1949–1976*, CPC Archives Publishing House, Edition 2013, Page 267.

11 [Poland] Oskar Lange, *Economic Theories of Socialism*, translated by Wang Hongchang, China Social Sciences Publishing House, Edition 1981.

12 Karl Marx, *Critique of Political Economics (Manuscripts of 1857–1858)*, *Selections of Marx and Engels*, Vol. 30, People's Publishing House, Edition 1995, Page 106.

13 Karl Marx, Introduction to *Critique of Political Economics*. Vol. 2 of *Selections of Marx and Engels*, People's Publishing House, Edition 2012, Page 699.

4 Logic of gradual reform in China

I. Introduction: different explanations to experiences on gradual reform

In the late 1980s and the early 1990s, two completely different roads for transition from the traditional planned economy to the market economy had shown up – i.e., the gradual reform in China and radical reform in the Soviet Union and Eastern European countries. When drastic changes in the Soviet Union and Eastern European countries occurred, western orthodox economists immediately reached a consensus that the radical method must be applied for the transition to the market economy, and the gradual reform could hardly succeed, as a wide gap could not be crossed by two steps. Based on the consensus, some basic propositions on economic transition were generated:

(1) Socialism and the market economy are incompatible, and the experiment on the market socialism has failed.
(2) Institutional transformation could not succeed unless the macro-economy is stable.
(3) Enterprises could hardly give an effective response to the market signal unless the private ownership is established.
(4) Enterprises' pursuit for profits would not lead to society satisfaction unless the price is determined by the market.
(5) The economic growth would be severely impeded unless it is fundamentally incorporated in the world economic system.
(6) The transition from the planned economy to the market economy must be rapid.
(7) The democratic political system is a necessary condition for the success of economic reform.[1]

The earlier propositions constitute the theoretical foundation for radical reform and "Big Bang" and play the dominant role in economic theories and policies at the beginning of transition. Theories of radical reform believe in the efficiency of a free market and hold that the strict demand retrenchment, deregulation, trade liberalization and privatization could promote economic growth. Therefore, the overall and rapid reform strategy should be applied to the transition to the market economy, and a wide gap could not be crossed by two steps. The slow progress and many trials – i.e. the gradual reform in China, would never go anywhere in the end. The voices of "China Collapse Theory" and "China Bashing" had risen one after another overseas and even domestically. These opinions of orthodox economists had been widely promoted by the International Monetary Fund and World Bank (WB), and the strong discourse power of mainstream textbooks on neoclassical economics, and they have become practical policies of transitional countries to a great extent.

However, the results of practices go beyond all expectations. Economists failed to predict the significant decline of production after price liberalization and macro-stabilization, benefits to "insiders" due to privatization, the dramatic growth of organizational criminal activities, severe so-called Mafia phenomenon in Russia, collapse of so many countries and, most unexpectedly, success of Chinese economic reform.[2] The gradual reform in China did not stop, and Chinese economy ushered in rapid growth, compared to the constant stagnation and decline of economies of the former Soviet Union and Eastern European countries, particularly former states of the Soviet Union.[3]

Countries that resorted to western mainstream theories for transition and development had failed, while the few countries that violated against those theories during the course of transition and development had succeeded. This is because the theories of social sciences come from the summary of social and economic phenomena, and the theories of social and economic phenomena summarized from developed countries are never the truth applicable everywhere.[4] As stated by Joseph E. Stigliz, it would be too irresponsible if we do not attempt to draw lessons since the difference between success and failure is too large.[5] The "Washington Consensus" based on neoliberalism theories was widely criticized due to the contrast between theories and practices, compared to the concern of and praise to the road of gradual reform in China. However, until now, western mainstream economists have focused on the transition method when analyzing the gradual reform in China and radical reform in the Soviet Union and Eastern Europe. They deny the significance of experiences on gradual reform in China and believe that the success of the gradual reform in China benefits from a series of favorable initial conditions, or attribute experiences on gradual reform in China to some special methods of marketization including partial reform, outside-system breakthroughs, spontaneous evolution and separation between economic reform and political reform but deny the fundamental difference between the essence and goal of reform between the gradual reform in China and radical reform in the former Soviet Union and Eastern Europe. However, the essence and goal exactly form the core issue for the selection and generation of the reform road. The method of reform is endogenous in the reform goal. Without the goal and essence of reform, the cost and profit of reform and the selection of the reform method would have no meaning.

Actually, the fundamental difference between China's gradual reform and the Soviet Union's radical reform lie in not the manner of marketization they adopted but in the essence and goal of reform. The goal of the gradual reform in China is to improve the socialist system and combine the basic socialist system with the market economy, while the goal of the radical reform in the Soviet Union and Eastern European countries is to fundamentally deny the socialist system, and establish the capitalist market economy. This constitutes the fundamental cause for the emergence of two different reform roads during the transition from the planned economy state to the market economy state in the late 1980s and the early 1990s. The success of China's gradual reform lies in that it had managed to find a specific way of combining the socialist economic system, political system, ideology and market economy together while taking into consideration the practical conditions of China. It is of great significance to pay attention to the following links in order to master China's experience and logic in its gradual reform.

II.   Constitutional system and reform road

One important question that we shall first clarify is the essence of the gradual reform in China. Until now, western mainstream economists have focused on the transition method when analyzing the gradual reform in China and radical reform in the Soviet Union and Eastern Europe. They deny the significance of experiences on gradual reform in China and believe that the success of the gradual reform in China benefits from a series of favorable initial conditions, or attribute experiences on gradual reform in China to some special methods of marketization including partial reform, outside-system breakthroughs, spontaneous evolution and separation between economic reform and political reform but deny the fundamental difference between the essence and goal of reform between the gradual reform in China and radical reform in the former Soviet Union and Eastern Europe. However, the essence and goal exactly form the core issue for the selection and generation of the reform road. The method of reform is endogenous in the reform goal. Without the goal and essence of reform, the cost and profit of reform and the selection of the reform method would have no meaning. From the perspective of the practical reform process, the major difference between the gradual reform in China and radical reform in the Soviet Union and Eastern Europe is caused by the different attitude of the social group leading different countries to the reform goal and the socialist constitutional system after the drastic changes in the Soviet Union and Eastern Europe in 1989 instead of a different arrangement of the speed, method and sequence of marketization or the specific methods such as whether the Reform is conducted in one step or several steps, is promoted wholly or partially, or compulsorily or induced, focuses on economic reform or political reform, resorts to incremental reform or storage reform, establishes first before destruction or destroys first before construction or starts from rural area or urban area. Different constitutional systems decide the differentiation of reform roads. In terms of transition of the social structure, the selection of the constitutional system is much more important than the institutional arrangement. The essence of the constitutional system and the direction and approach of the change make the core issue of economic transition, because of the follows:

(1) The content of the constitutional system decides the content of the system arrangements. The constitutional system is a basic social system, the rule to formulate rules. Different constitutional systems necessarily lead to numerous differences in specific institutional arrangements. The gradual reform in China is conducted based on the socialist constitutional system, which adheres to the dominant role of public ownership (once adhered to the principle of planned economy as the dominant role in the early stage of reform) in terms of the economic system, adheres to the leadership by the Communist Party in the political system and adheres to Marxism-Leninism, Mao Zedong Thought and the socialist theoretical system with Chinese characteristics in ideology. In the premise, it gradually reforms the traditional economic system, political system and ideology, introduces in non-public economies. Develops socialist democracy, reforms the traditional ideology and realizes the transition from the planned economy to the market economy. The radical reform in the Soviet Union and Eastern Europe fundamentally denied the socialist constitutional system and transited to the western-style free economy or personal capitalist system in an all-around way, which necessarily emphasized on economic privatization and political and ideological diversity in content of reform.

(2) The change method of the constitutional system decides the way of reform. The progressivity of reform mainly refers to the change method of the institutional system instead of the speed of marketization. The fundamental characteristic of the gradual reform lies in that it does not hold the "revolutionary" attitude to overturn and reconstruct the original constitutional system, but gradually revises the content of the original constitutional system by marginal adjustments and gives new definition to the socialist system. For example, the traditional socialist economic system was based on the planned economy, while the current system is linked to the market economy, and the traditional socialist economic theories believed that the state ownership is the advanced form of the socialist ownership and other ownership forms should be transformed to this form, while the report of the 15th National Congress of the CPC put forward that the leading role of the state ownership was manifested by its control instead of its proportion, and the appropriate decline of the proportion of state ownership does not affect the essence of the socialist system. The gradual "correction" of the constitutional system necessarily leads to moderate and consecutive reform, while the radical reform completely denies the original socialist constitutional system and thus requires complete and fundamental reform, leading to the institutional gap between the new and old system.

(3) The constitutional system specifies the conditions and basic rules for collective selection and thus directly influences the cost of the political system and method to apply public power for institutional innovation.[6] In other

words, the constitutional system decides the structure of the institutional game or the "process of reform". Under different game structures, different stakeholders participating in the Reform have different rights, positions, ways of act, and game strategies in the institutional selection. The "process of reform" is like the "voting process" in the public choice, which largely decides the reform method and further decides the reform results.[7] In terms of the process of reform, the gradual reform is carried out based on the relatively concentrated non-diversified political structure. The political structure creates necessary conditions for implementation of steady and controlled gradual reform. Once this political order was denied and the western-style political diversity was applied, political conditions for the gradual reform would be damaged, and the decisions of reform would not be controlled by the top-down political structure but would rely on the open contest by different interest groups in the political market. Briefly speaking, the reform goal of China is to establish the socialist market economy and conduct reform of marketization based on the socialist constitutional system, while the radical reform in the Soviet Union and Eastern Europe fundamentally deny the socialist constitutional system. As concluded by Janos Kornai, their difference is not about the method and speed of transition or the moderate or fierce status of the Reform, but is actually about whether it is a reform or the so-called revolution, or, according to Jeffrey Sachs and Yang Xiaokai et al., about the essence of constitutionalism.[8]

Therefore, different constitutional systems constitute the fundamental cause for the emergence of two transformation methods at the late 1980s. The particularity of the essence and goal of the gradual reform in China determines a series of specific characteristics of the reform method, such as the combination of the compulsory implementation from top to bottom and induced changes from bottom to top, wide application of the dual-track system of administrative coordination and market coordination, adherence to the major role of the public ownership and active development of multiple forms of ownership, emphasis on mutual coordination of reform, development and stability and economic marketization and separation from the western-style political diversity. These characteristics can only be accurately explained when the essence and goal of economic transformation of China are correctly mastered.

III. Goal and process

People often define construction of the market economy as a large systematic project. This is not accurate as it simplifies the work. Practically, different from building roads or houses, construction of the market economy needs a precise and detailed construction drawing in advance, and different from producing certain material products, it must follow a fixed process. The market economy, as the reform goal, is a complicated social system. Following features shall be mastered to understand the complicated system:

(1) Integrity. Superficially, the market system seems to be an economic system for resources allocation with price as the core. However, the price is based on the value, and the value reflects the free exchange relation between economic entities of independent property right. Without reform of the ownership system, the price signal has no way to play its part. Moreover, the fundamental reform of the ownership system requires the complete market of production factors, a complete legislation system and a relatively complete social security system, as well as corresponding political, legal, ideological and cultural atmosphere. All these factors are fundamentally based on the development of social productive forces. The market economy has been developed from a lower level to a higher level driven by increasing economic surplus, rich social demands, improvement of people's capability, wide social division of labor and technology and product innovation. Therefore, the transition to the market economy not only involves transformation of the method of resources allocation but also incorporates the long-term and complicated overall process in social, economic, political and cultural area.

(2) Historicalness. The market economy is not a certain facility or tool that could survive without the specific social structure or that could be moved around a different institutional environment and historical conditions. On the contrary, the market economic systems in different historical stages and social structures show a different institutional environment, technical foundation and cultural background, and share both similarities and differences. The classical market economy is different with the modern market economy; the model of UK and America is not the model in Northern Europe, and the model in East Asia presents its unique characteristics. The experiment on marketization in China by now is carried out under restrictions of industrialization and the socialist Constitution; the reform goal is to build socialism, and later the reform is encountered with challenges of globalization and informatization. The profound historical background renders special historical connotation to the market economy of China.

(3) Uncertainty. The market economy is historical and thus is not fixed. It necessarily changes along with the changes of subjective and objective conditions. In China, the reform goal was not originally confirmed as the socialist market economy, but was established based on constant reform practices. Since 1979, the reform goal of China has experienced several development stages, from "the planned economy as the mainstay and the market regulation as the complementary approach", planned commodity economy to the "government regulating the market and market guiding enterprises". After 1992, the market-oriented reform has been clearly defined as the construction of the socialist market economic system. Even so, this goal fails to solve all issues for good and all but can only be gradually improved through constant explorations and tests.

Someone may propose that since we have already confirmed on the reform goal of the market economy, the remaining problem should be no other than seeking for the best reform path under confirmed conditions and goal and attaining the reform goal with the full speed within the shortest time, so, since the starting point and the goal of reform are fixed, why we do not resort to the one-step radical reform strategy but proceed in an orderly way and step by step and why there are differences between the gradual reform and radical reform. First, it shall be pointed out that the starting point of reform varies in different countries. Even in original planned-economy countries in the Soviet Union, Eastern Europe and China, the starting points of reform present distinct differences. The reform goals in different countries such as China, the Soviet Union and Eastern European counties are not only different but also undefined. The socialist market economy as the reform goal is a new kind of market economic system in human history. The system can only be gradually established and improved through constant practices, and people can understand and recognize it only after a long historical period. Moreover, if we transfer the perspective of understanding from the method of marketization and partial institutional transition to evolution of the overall social structure and constitutional system, it is found that as an overall process of social transition, reform is not an economic calculation pursuing the maximum or minimum value, but a complicated historical course full of choices and creation. This is because of the follows:

(1) The social system is a complicated organic system, and evolution of the society is unique and irreversible with evident uncertainty and changeability. Therefore, it is impossible for people to make an accurate design of the reform goal and implement such design without any error. The transition to the market economy incorporates many trials or attributes of evolutionism.
(2) Fundamentally, the formation of the reform road is the result of mutual effect among the economic, political and cultural system of the social structure and the game among different individuals and different interest groups with the goal to maximize their own benefits under certain conditions. This is a course of typical social choice, which necessarily varies in different countries and different social structures.
(3) The past and the present, and the present and the future are closely linked to each other, while the fixed social structure and social conditions, as the historical precipitation, may dramatically restrict people's choice and freedom of action. This is so-called path dependence phenomenon. Since different countries see different initial conditions for reform, their specific paths of reform definitely show differences.

In short, the transition from the planned economy to the market economy in China is not only the change of the method of resources allocation but also a course of social transformation consisting of profound social economic, political and cultural changes and full of conflicts, contradictions, creations and destructions accompanied with three major historical changes, industrialization, modernization and reform of the socialist Constitution system. This process must be long-term, complicated and hard and can never be realized just through "control over currency and release of control over price". This constitutes the fundamental cause for the gradual realization of economic reform in China.

IV. From top to bottom and from bottom to top

The institutional changes are divided into two types according to the subject of the change – i.e. the compulsory change and the induced change. The induced change refers to the spontaneous change when a group of people respond to the opportunities in making profits resulting from an imbalanced system, while the compulsory change refers to the change imposed by the act of government.[9] The former one is from top to bottom, while the latter one is from bottom to top, and the former one is spontaneous and evolutionary, and the latter one is self-conscious and constructed. The radical reform is a kind of typical compulsory change, which pre-designs the market economic system with the western developed capitalist countries as an ideal model, formulates the "package" reform proposal according to the design and implements it from top to bottom through the act of government. The gradual reform makes full use of the active role of spontaneous reform and the initiative of the grassroots units, advocates bold innovation and trial and perfectly integrates the compulsory and induced changes and evolutionary rationality and constructed rationality.

The Reform in China is first a kind of compulsory reform led by the government. Under the framework of the socialist constitutional system, the evolution course of the socialist system requires more rationality, organization and control than capitalism. Particularly at the initial stage of development of the market economy, policies and decrees of the Party and government largely lead the direction and path of reform, so the Reform in China presents the evident government-based feature. However, the characteristic and success of the Reform in China lie in not the pure compulsoriness but the combination of compulsory and induced change. It is an important lesson of the gradual reform in China to make full use of the role of spontaneous reform and the initiative of the grassroots units. Though the Reform is initiated from top to bottom, it only recognizes the reform requirements that have already existed in social life; the Reform is conducted under unified leadership, but the reform measures, content and steps of different specific departments, regions and units are diversified; the reform advocates bold innovation and trial, consciously allows, permits or tacitly approves partially "breaking the rules" or "going beyond the rules" and widely spreads any act that proves to be rational by practices; individuals, enterprises and other grassroots units exert unprecedented initiative and creation in the institutional innovation in order to realize maximum interests; and the perfect design, accurate calculation and overall planning have often been left behind by practices before their generation. It is of greater instructional significance to resort to more trials and go on the road step by step. The practice of the contract responsibility system in the rural area can be considered as a typical example of the combination of the spontaneous induced reform and self-conscious compulsory reform.

As is known to all, the economic reform in China since 1979 started first from the rural area, while the breakthrough of reform in the rural area started from the household contract responsibility system in agriculture, which was actually not the new thing created after reform. In over two decades between collectivization of the rural area and the Third Plenary Session of the 11th Central Committee, the household contract responsibility system had been spontaneously carried out in large scale in the rural area in 1956 and 1961 and had been wholeheartedly supported by the broad masses of peasants as it met peasants' interests. However, due to dominance by the "left" line, it was criticized and inhibited as the "specter of capitalism". From autumn and winter of 1978 to spring of 1979, "fixing farm output quotas on the household basis" and "work contracted to households" emerged again in some places. As influenced by the principle of seeking truth from facts, this measure that theoretically violated against policies had been tacitly approved by the leading local authority in practice. People were holding the altitude of having a try and waiting for changes. As practice is the sole criterion for testing truth, the rapid development of agricultural production declared the success of the contract responsibility system. Since then, the spontaneous and decentralized induced changes had become the compulsory change promoted by the government from top to bottom, and the contract responsibility had been widely spread.

Major advantages of the Reform from bottom to top consist of the follows:

(1) The Reform in China, such a big country with vast land and complicated conditions, lacks existing experiences and mature theories, so the Reform implemented by the government from top to bottom may be encountered with huge risks due to insufficient information. When the grassroots units fully play their initiative in institutional innovation and adopt efficient measures based on practical conditions, it is possible to make full use of dispersed information resources, avoid major errors and reduce unnecessary losses.

(2) The spontaneous reform refers to the institutional innovation conducted when the subjects of reform pursue their personal interests and only takes place when the expected revenue of economic entities exceeds costs. From the perspective of single subjects, they would necessarily choose the institutional form that improves efficiency and competitiveness and changes those institutional forms of low efficiency that hinder play of their abilities in order to improve revenues from activities and respond to fierce market competition.

(3) The transition from the planned economy to the market economy is aimed at denying the top-to-bottom administration order and expanding freedom of enterprises and individuals in making choices. The transfer of the right in institutional choice from the centralized to the decentralized method and from government to grassroots units constitutes the necessary trend of reform. The relaxed and natural environment is provided for the growth of the new institution only by gradually expanding the freedom of grassroots units in

choosing institutions and allowing spontaneity, diversity and competition of institutional changes.

However, notices shall also be given to the evident weaknesses of overemphasizing the bottom-to-top reform. First, the overall macro-reform can only be carried out from top to bottom, such as the fiscal and tax system, financial system, foreign exchange system and basic systems. Second, due to the released budget constraints and distorted market mechanism, if purely emphasizing on releasing control in practices, it often fails to bring efficient competition and improve efficiency, but may deteriorate the market order and lower efficiency of resources allocation. We can easily find that the so-called reform in many departments, regions and enterprises is essentially only making profits and getting rich by turning the public wealth to private wealth and sacrificing overall interests, thus leading to severe corruption, unfair income and chaos in public order. Therefore, the Reform from top to bottom and reform from bottom to top could be integrated and should not be set against each other.

V. Overall reform and partial reform

Compared to the radical reform, the gradual reform in China is known as the partial or divisional reform, which changes the old system from every partial change and finally realizes the overall transition of the economic system. Divisional reforms consist of two different forms:

(1) The new and the old systems show succession in time. During the course of gradual reform, the new and the old systems are not separate or diametrically opposed, but present evident continuity and succession, while the transition between the two must experience many different stages, go through many intermediate links and adopt many intermediate forms. The goal of the Reform at the initial stage was to improve the planned economy and apply the guiding principle of leading role of the planned economy and the supplementary role of market regulation; after 1984, the planned commodity economy became the reform goal; and since 1992, the socialist market economic system has been confirmed as the reform goal. The reforms in specific departments and areas have also experienced corresponding process of changes. For example, the price reform has experienced three major stages: the state price adjustment in the initial stage of reform, the combination of adjustment and release of control after 1984 and focusing on release of control since 1992, and reform of state-owned enterprises has gone through three major stages, expansion of powers and transfer of profits in the initial stage of reform, the contracting system after 1986 and the modern enterprise system reform after 1992.

(2) The new and the old systems show compatibility in space. In the same period, different areas present evident differences in reform sequence and reform degree, forming the unique road of "encircling" the cities from the rural areas, "encircling" the coastal area from inland and "encircling"

state-owned economies from non-state-owned economies before finally realizing the overall transition of the economic system. For example, when the
urban economy was still subject to the collectively planned economic system
in the early 1980s, the Reform in the urban area in China succeeded and
attained great progress, while the market of production factors was still
under planned control. The commodity market in China led to the realization
of marketization in the middle and late 1980s, when the production, distribution and pricing of the majority of commodities were incorporated in the
market adjustment; the special economic zones in coastal areas were in line
with the international market and realized marketization to a large extent,
and, moreover, reforms in pricing, tax, finance, foreign trade, social security
and enterprises were also out of sync in time and space.

It is necessary for the gradual reform in China to apply the strategy of "developing from the partial to the overall reform".

(1) The Reform in China is conducted based on relatively stable constitutional
    system. The old system did not completely lose its practical rationality on
    the whole, and the new system was gradually generated on the basis of the
    old system.
(2) Compared to the planned economic system in the Soviet Union and Eastern
    Europe, the traditional system in China was more loose in internal structure
    and showed clear independence and difference.
(3) Due to lack of theories and experiences and restricted understanding of the
    reform goal and process, the Reform could only proceed from reality, move on
    step by step and make progress by solving specific problems one after another.

The radical reform, also known as the overall reform and "Big Bang", attempted
to realize transition from the planned economy to the market economy in a short
period by tightening the currency, releasing control over price and fully promoting
privatization, liberalization and opening. It is also not occasional for the Soviet
Union and Eastern European countries to resort to the radical reform and apply the
"Big Bang" theory for overall promotion.

(1) The radical reform thoroughly denied the socialist constitutional system.
    The traditional system here completely lost its foundation for existence and
    the new system emerged on the ruins of the old system.
(2) The traditional planned economic system was rigid and the conflicts accu-
    mulated in a long period were comprehensively intensified, so it lost the
    ability of self-renewal and partial adjustment.
(3) The capitalist market economy, as the reform goal, has mature theories and
    practices, so the overall reform is theoretically feasible.

Theories of the radical reform were mainly derived from the neoclassical economics, which assumed that all people pursued for maximum interests despite

different social, cultural and historical environment, and resources could freely flow and the market economy could be formed only by abolishing the planned economy. Theories of the radical reform also believe that the market system is a whole, its factors cannot be separately introduced, and it only plays its role when it satisfies all conditions including free enterprises, free prices, competitive market environment and macro-control, and partial reform only brings about partial success. For example, the stability of the macro-economy is the prerequisite for releasing control over prices, the role of the pricing mechanism requires innovation of the system of property rights; the innovation of the property rights system requires reform of the legal and political system, and enterprises, market and price, government finance, finance, salary and pricing reform constitute an integral whole of mutual connection and shall be wholly promoted. According to this idea, the new and the old systems are broken in time and mutually excluded against each other in space, and it is better when the time for transition between the old and the new system is shorter and the intermediate links are fewer.

Though the earlier theories seem scientific, they are not correct, because recognition of the universal connection worldwide does not deny the relative independence of things. For example, in a general sense, the adjusting role of price in resources allocation is only realized under rigid budget restraint, so the release of control over price shall be carried out simultaneously with hardening of budget restraint of enterprises. However, the problem lies in that enterprises in reality consist of different types of enterprises, the markets in reality consist of different types of markets, and different enterprises, different markets and their mutual relations are partially different. For example, the opening of the market of agricultural products is closely related to behaviors of farmers and consumers but has nothing to do directly with whether state-owned steel plants assume sole responsibility for their own profits or losses, and whether the farmers assume sole responsibility for their own profits or losses is closely related to marketization of the price of agricultural products but has no relation to the opening of the steel price. Therefore, the integrity of the economic system does not mean that all reform measures shall be carried out simultaneously or shall have no difference in time and space. On the contrary, the application of divisional reform better complies with laws of development of things and is more rational.

(1) It would be easier to attain real effect by starting from reform of departments of lower reform cost and higher benefits due to lower obstruction and greater benefits. For example, the Reform in China started from reform of the contract system in rural area instead of core departments of the traditional planned economy, which aroused the enthusiasm of peasants, promoted agricultural production and won great success. Enterprise reform first started from expansion of powers and transfer of profits, introduced in the market relation against small resistance, solved the problem of insufficient driving force of enterprises and acquired great profits in all aspects.

(2) Some divisions leading in reform and achieving success may give rise to a domino effect and promote reform of other divisions. For example, the

success of reform in the rural area rendered the broad market, sufficient labors and rich agricultural products for cities, thus promoting reform and development of urban economy; development of non-state-owned economies created the market environment of competition and new development opportunities, thus promoting reform of state-owned economies, and Reform and Opening Up and economic development in coastal areas further drove reform and development of inland.

(3) Arrange for the reform sequence from the easier to the more advanced, which can gradually break down reform difficulties and lower reform risks. Since different parts of the new institution require different conditions and time for development, so reform may be relatively more difficult or easier. If reforms of different difficulties were carried out at the same time, parts of the reforms in the lack of conditions would necessarily result in chaos and hinder the whole economic reform and development. On the contrary, if the links between systems were loose and the content and sequence of reform were relatively independent, different parts of the economic system could change to adapt to their respective environment and realize the favorable relationship between mutual adaption and mutual promotion.

Without a doubt, the difference between the partial reform and the overall reform is relative. Different parts of the radical reform may also have some differences in time and space, while the gradual reform is not simply adding independent parts together. The part and the whole are always in a unity despite their differences.

VI.   Dual-track transition

The dual-track transition is a typical form of the gradual reform. In the gradual reform, the new and the old systems are not completely opposite to each other but are compatible to a certain degree; they are not broken but are successive. The old system does not completely lose the rationality for existence due to reform, and the new system gradually grows when the old system is still playing its part, and the existing interest structure shall maintain relative stability and the new interest relationship is generated through marginal adjustment. In the gradual reform in China, the new and the old are not clearly divided but have an indistinct border. For example, in western economics on transition, the leadership of the Communist Party, state-owned enterprises, sovereignty of labor and planned regulation are all factors of the old system and shall be resolutely cleared. However, in China, these factors are essential requirements of the socialist system and are incorporated in the framework of the new system. In this way, we can clearly see the lack of reality of the radical reform of whole advancement and the one-step process in China. Under these restraints, it is impossible to realize the transition of the economic system at one step. As the evitable outcome of the gradual reform, the new and the old systems would coexist, conflicts, integrates and alternates for a long time.

Among various types of dual-track systems, the dual-track price system is the representative one. The so-called dual-track price system refers to two different forms of the market price and the planned price of the same commodity in the same market at the same time. The dual-track price system has existed in the history for a long time but was concealed in the fissure of the planned economy before reform. Along with the implementation of the reform of expansion of powers and transfer of profits in 1984, the State Council allowed the floating of 20% of the sale of products by enterprises for the part of overproduction. In January 1985, the government provided that the price of the industrial means of production for the part of overproduction could be freely fixed, and, since then, the dual-track price system had been officially confirmed and promoted to some other departments. Later on, the proportion of the market price was increasing and has finally become the major form of the price system. The dual-track system is the most distinctive form of reform in China. In addition to the price reform, it has penetrated all aspects including the enterprise reform, division reform, ownership reform, foreign exchange reform and fiscal reform, etc. From perspectives of the overall pattern of the economic system, the dual-track system can be concluded as following categories:

(1) The dual-track system of price and market: refers to the dual-track system of the market of production factors including the commodity price, salary, interest rate, foreign exchange rate and land price and pricing.
(2) The dual-track system of ownership: mainly consists of two different ownership forms, the state-owned and non-state-owned economies.
(3) The dual-track system of the division structure: refers to the major difference in the reform degree of different divisions and co-existence of marketized divisions and non-marketized divisions.
(4) The dual-track system of the regional structure: refers to different marketization degree in different regions, with marketization in coastal regions more advanced in coastal areas than the inland and marketization in developed regions more advanced in backward regions.

People always hold different opinions on the position and role of the dual-track system. However, despite all these evaluations of its advantages and disadvantages, a fact that cannot be denied is that the dual-track system is not the result of people's subjective imagination, but the natural choice in practical reform by practices. The application of the dual-track transition, on the one hand, maintains relative stability of the existing economic system, economic order and interest relations and guarantees normal economic operation, and, on the other hand, gradually introduces in the new economic system, provides the new driving force mechanism, information mechanism and regulation mechanism for economic development and improves efficiency of resources allocation. The application of the dual-track transition means the long-term dual-track economies of co-existence of the new and old system, and the old system will continue to play its role in a relatively long period. Theoretically, it would lower the efficiency of resources allocation and may lead to the return of the old system. However, any system is generated and plays its role under certain conditions. The planned system also found its historical rationality for existence and the growth of the market system demands certain social conditions. The dual system is the efficient system during the transition period. From the new evolutionary perspective, there is no choice if there is no diversity, and the rapid change to institutions and organizations always sacrifices efficiency. On the contrary, the existence of the old system and the frictions during the institutional change would maintain the diversity of institutions, provide a wide range of space for selection and generation of new systems and thus promote the growth of new systems.

VII.   Relation between stability and growth

The common problem of the planned economic system lies in the lack of commodities and price distortion. Along with adjustment to price and release of control during reform, the general price level would necessarily rise by a wide margin. Therefore, stability of the macro-economy is essential to economic transition. The gradual reform in China and the radical reform in the Soviet Union and the Eastern Europe also show great differences in how to realize stability of the macro-economy.

The macro-policies in the radical reform are also generally called "shock treatment", which attempts to realize the transition to the market economy in a short period by implementing strict economic contraction, eliminating the excess demand in economic life, releasing the control over the price of commodities and production factors, forming competitive markets and facilitating bankruptcy and recombination of state-owned enterprises. These countries applied the "shock treatment" mainly due to the following reasons:

(1) Before the radical reform in 1989, the Soviet Union and Eastern European countries suffered severe imbalance in the economic structure, increasingly intensified inflation and macro-economy close to a breakdown and must adopt strict economic contraction.
(2) On the one hand, the radical reform resulted in violent turbulence in economic order and economic relations, and, on the other hand, it fundamentally denied the planned economy, which excluded the possibility of applying the administrative control to eliminating the inflation and made the strict demand retrenchment the only choice to solve inflation.
(3) Advocators of "shock treatment" believe in neoclassicism. The theory holds that the adjustment to production factors is instant without any friction and inflation is a pure currency phenomenon at any time, so the free economy can be established and the resources can be rationally allocated if eliminating the excessive currency and removing restraints by the planned economy. The "shock treatment" had incurred disastrous consequences in many countries. Since this drastic monetary deflation emerged along with violent changes of economic structure, serious crack of economic mechanism and evidently growing uncertainty of economic behaviors, thus, it is different from the general economic contraction and postwar conditions of Japan and West Germany, but it

formed an economic recession different from the general economic cycle which was called the "transition recession" by Kornai.[10] Its severity had far gone beyond people's expectation and even exceeded the Great Depression in the 1930s.

Different with the "shock treatment", the gradual reform in China has been carried out based on relatively stable constitutional system, interest structure and economic order, and the basic macro-economy goal of the government is to realize the constant and rapid economic development. Therefore, when formulating policies on the macro-economy, the government not only considers demands on stabilization but also considers the mutual coordination among reform, development and stability; it not only thinks about the total volume but also thinks about the mutual relation among the total volume, structure and system. The macro-policy of gradualism formed upon comprehensive consideration of demand, supply, structure and administrative coordination has maintained the constant and rapid economic growth and avoided the severe recession brought about by the "shock treatment". Advantages of this kind of policies include the follows:

(1) The rapid economic development can significantly increase the national income, create more employment opportunities, improve the capability of the government, enterprises, individuals and other economic entities to adapt themselves to reform, prevent the social unrest incurred due to bankruptcy, unemployment and income decline and render favorable material foundation for in-depth implementation of reform.
(2) The gradual reform is realized by the incremental reform driving the storage reform. The rapid economic development can create wide space for the incremental reform, realize rapid growth of the proportion of the new system and provide material compensation to the reform to the old system and create a favorable social environment.
(3) As the Reform is carried out based on relatively stable constitutional order, it gains the benefits brought by the new system, meanwhile it maintains the succession of the old and the new system in transition; reduces the cost of system transition and structure adjustment; makes full use of the material resources, human resources; organization resources and information resources already formed; and improves efficiency of resources allocation.
(4) By facilitating economic development during the process of reform, it enables various reform measures to achieve evident results in a shorter period, shortens the time lag between the "input" and "output" of the Reform, promotes all areas' trust in reform and realizes the virtuous cycle between reform and development.

The core idea of the radical reform can be concluded as "controlling the currency and releasing the control over the price", which creates conditions for marketization reform through stabilized macro-policies. However, the possibility shall be taken into consideration of tight money in addition to the necessity, while the economic reform shall consider both the stability of the aggregate price level and demands on constant growth of the national economy. In conclusion, the idea of "control the currency and release the control over the price" exists following defects:

(1) The tight money not only lowers the price but also reduce the output. Particularly, in the process of the gradual reform, the institutional transition needs a long historical process. The application of the long-term deflation policy would necessarily lead to long-term recession, which cannot be borne by any country.
(2) The transition to the market economy is an overall issue on institutional innovation, with marketization of the price as an aspect. The goal of economic transition can hardly be realized even the control over the price is released under conditions of the softened restraints on enterprise budget, weak development of the market system and severe imbalance of the economic structure.
(3) The quantity of currency supply is not completely decided by the subjective wishes of the currency management authority and the government but is largely determined by objective requirements of the operating mechanism and operating status of the national economy. In terms of the process of formulation of macro-policies, it is not a complete exogenous variable but is also an endogenous variable to a great extent.

Some scholars often advocated the feasibility of "control the currency and release the control over the price" based on experiences in the West Germany and Japan after the war. However, the economic reform in China and the transition from the controlled economy to the market economy in West Germany and Japan are fundamentally different. The two countries were originally applying the private ownership and the market economy but had to resort to strict centralized management over economy due to the war, so the transition from the controlled economy to the market economy was merely an issue about policies or environment but did not constitute innovation of the fundamental institution. On the contrary, in China, the key issue is exactly the institutional innovation and the structural adjustment instead of merely a pure macro-policy issue, which is impossible to be completed by releasing the control over the price within a short term.

In the transition period, the macro-economic policies of China have different goals compared to the countries of advanced market economy and show great differences with western countries' market economies in terms of implementation measures, role and process. In the west, the macro-issue is mainly the issue on aggregate, and the macro-economic policies are mainly policies on aggregate, while the structure and institution are basically not involved, or, in other words, the western macro-economic policies are carried out based on prerequisites of developed market mechanism and demand constraint economy and the resources allocation are completely conducted based on price regulation. However, in China, the macro-issue is not only one issue but also the issue on the structure and institution, which can only be solved through coordination of three aspects, the aggregate, structure and system. As the aggregate, structure and system issues have close relation to each other, the macro-economic policies must fully consider the special condition and integrate the issues on aggregate, structure and system. To further explain the meaning of the policy integrating aggregate, structure and system, it puts the macro-economic policies under the dual system led by the government and perfectly combines the planned regulation and market regulation, indirect regulation and direct regulation, aggregate policy and structure policy, macro-management and micro-management, long-term policies and short-term policies and reform, development and stability. It realizes economic development and the reform goal of the economic system in the relatively stable environment and perfectly integrates reform, development and stability.

VIII.   In-system reform and out-system reform

The ownership reform constitutes the core line of the economic reform, while the goal and method of the ownership reform make the major difference between the gradual reform and radical reform.

The core of the radical reform is privatization in a large scale. Privatization is the economic as well as the political requirement for the radical reform.[11] The goal of the radical reform can only be reached after realizing privatization of the public ownership. Though economists hold different opinions on the method and speed of privatization and countries in transition vary in specific measures on this issue, generally, it has become a common sense of the radical reform to realize privatization as soon as possible. According to them, rapid privatization could complete the goal of transformation quickly, prevent the return of the old system, eliminate economic uncertainties, guarantee the balance of budget and favor social equality.[12]

The economic reform in China is carried out based on the basic economic system at the primary stage of socialism. Since the Reform and Opening Up, the Communist Party of China has formulated the principle of keeping public ownership as the mainstay of the economy and allowing diverse forms of ownership to develop side by side and confirmed this principle as the basic economic system at the primary stage of socialism, which has laid the foundation for the combination of socialism and the market economy. Through three decades of in-depth reform, the majority of the state-owned enterprises in China have become independent business entities facing the market, and despite rapid development of diverse economic ownership, state-owned enterprises, particularly the large and medium-sized state-owned enterprises, are still playing the leading role in many key sectors. In the rural area, the double management system combining centralization and decentralization with household contracting operation as the basis guarantees the principal status of peasants in the market, maintains the collective ownership of land and promotes constant development of the rural economy.

By combining development of the public ownership as the mainstay and the common development of diverse ownership, the reform of the ownership structure in China walks out a special road integrating the in-system reform and out-system breakthrough. It is noted that the success of the gradual reform in China largely profits from rapid development of diverse ownership forms particularly the non-state-owned economies. It is too difficult to start marketization purely from reform of the state ownership due to various weaknesses of the traditional state owner-ship such as the difficulty for enterprises to go bankrupt, the difficulty for work-ers to lose jobs, the difficulty to separate politics from enterprises and too heavy historical burden. Meanwhile, development of non-state-owned economies could overcome these difficulties, create the complete market relation and competitive market environment, vigorously promote generation and development of the mar-ket economy and actively facilitate reform of state-owned enterprises. This kind of role of non-state-owned economies in the economic transition is concluded as the out-system breakthrough by some scholars. However, when emphasizing the active role of out-system reform, the great role of state-owned economies in reform and development cannot be ignored. First, the primary status of public ownership and the leading role of the state-owned economy guarantee the socialist attributes of reform. Second, the leading role of the state-owned economy is favorable for the stable, coordinated and constant development of the national economy. Third, the perfect combination of the state-owned economy and market economy is a key to establishment and development of the socialist market economy. The goal of the establishment of the socialist market economy can hardly be realized if purely relying on the out-system breakthrough of non-state-owned economies without in-depth reform within the state-owned economic system. Therefore, the in-system reform and out-system breakthrough cannot be set against each other, and the combination of the reform of the state-owned economy and the promotion of the development of the non-state-owned economy is exactly the fundamental experi-ence of the success of the gradual reform in China.

IX.   Centralization and decentralization

The relation between the central government and local government is an important theoretical and practical issue in marketization reform. Generally, the market mech-anism is linked to the decentralized decision making, while the planned regulation is indispensable from the centralized decision making by the central government. Therefore, regarding the relationship between the central and local government, liberals are often inclined to decentralization and believe that decentralization is favorable to individual freedom and market competition, while nationalists mostly endorse centralization and believe that centralization is favorable to safeguarding national interests and unifying the market. More people are seeking for certain balance between centralization and decentralization. Different opinions about cen-tralization and decentralization are all reflected in transition economics.

During economic reform in China, the local government plays a special but important role and attracts high attention from scholars. Jean C. Oi names the acts of local government after the fiscal responsibility reform as local government corporatization corporatism. This model promotes local economic development,

retains the strong leadership of the government and avoids privatization and economic collapse as that happened in the Soviet Union and Eastern Europe.[13] Qian
Yingyi et al. believe that the success of Chinese reform mainly profits from the M
structure of the traditional system – i.e., the "block" structure of multiple levels
and multiple regions based on the regional principle. In the M organization, the
grassroots government has greater autonomy, and the relation between regions is
market-oriented. This structure weakens the administrative control, strengthens
market activities and stimulates development of non-state-owned enterprises. They
also name this reform model as "the reform model from federalism in Chinese
style to privatization in Chinese style".[14] Yang Ruilong thinks that the institutional
change in China has successively experienced three stages, the supply orientation,
central diffusion and demand orientation, during the transition of China to the
market economy. In the central diffusion stage of the institutional change, the local
government plays the key role.[15]

Some other scholars emphasize more on the negative role of decentralization
during marketization. As early as in the late 1980s, the criticism against "duke
economy" and "administrative decentralization" had emerged, which considered
that, on the one hand, the administrative decentralization was of features of the
planned economy and even strengthened the administrative control over enterprises and market in many aspects, and, on the other hand, it made the local government the market entity that pursued maximum benefits, which was a halfway
marketization reform as a result of unchecked construction, repeated construction, investment inflation and regional blockade, etc., affected the macro-control,
hindered formation of the uniform market and even led to greater corruption.[16] In
the early 1990s, particularly around the implementation of reform of tax-sharing
system, the criticism against the "duke economy" culminated and an influential
idea was formed. The idea believed that the financial resources of the central government had been lowered to the lowest level at that time, the pattern of "weak central government and strong local government" had been formed, and the national
unity faced danger, so it was necessary to improve the capability of the central
government and inhibit expansion of the local strength. This idea also considered
it necessary to give full play to the leading role of the central government during
the transition to the market economy, mainly because voluntary transactions could
not take place in a system vacuum; the market mechanism could not automati-
cally show up, and the market transition was a process full of conflicts. It demonstrated an idea of Polanyi that under the prerequisite of constantly expanding
centralized interventionism, the free market was explored and was not closed since
then.[17] Olivier Blanchard believes that the local government is the driving force
for economic growth in China, but the local government plays a negative role in
Russia, mainly because of the different political centralization degree. In Russia,
the central government exerts very limited control and is incapable to stop local
governments gaining profits from taxation, rent-seeking and control. However, in
China, the centralized political structure enables the central government to enforce
abundant rewards and punishments and effectively restrict this kind of behaviors
by local government.[18]

The earlier two opposite opinions both make sense to a certain degree, but the actual conditions are more complicated. In practices, decentralization may become the driving force and obstruction for marketization, and centralization is also double edged. The concrete analysis is required.

First, it shall be admitted that despite the great advantages of centralization, it lacks freedom and creation and cannot adapt to the development of the market civilization and modernization. The transition from the planned economy to the market economy is a process of transfer from the centralized to decentralized economic and political power and from unification to diversification. From this perspective, as decentralization, market economy and democratic politics have internal connections, giving full play to the local government is favorable for the development of the market economy and democratic politics and realizing economic and social modernization as soon as possible. However, we cannot, therefore, deny the necessity of proper centralization and mechanically copy federalism of American style. In addition to the requirements of the socialist constitutional system and the historical stage of China now, understanding the following fact would help us understand the significance of centralization. The fact is that the great organization and mobilization ability of the central government, the political tradition of authoritarianism and the traditional culture with the group value as the core have been recognized as the major factor contributing to the success of modernization of East Asian countries including China, which are the precious institutional resources of values beyond measurement left by the brilliant civilizations of over thousands of years and enable the East Asian model to last longer than the model of West Asia, South Asia, Latin America and even Eastern Europe. Practically, the key to this issue is not the choice between centralization or decentralization or the pure right separation between the central and local government; we are facing an overall and historical issue; rebuilding the relation between the central and local government under the historical background of industrialization, informatization, marketization and globalization; and realizing economic and social modernization, which is a brand-new historical mission.

X. Reform and opening up

The modern market system has developed from two different transition roads. One is the endogenous change, the transition road of the Western Europe, and the other is exogenous change, the transition road of the majority of countries and regions other than the Western Europe.[19] The endogenous road of marketization was driven by the internal forces and gradually realized the transition to the modern market economy through spontaneous gradual reform from bottom to top after a long process of evolution. The exogenous road refers to the institutional transition to the market economy within a short period through fierce conflicts and violent changes upon the compulsory reform from top to bottom as stimulated and induced by external shock.

As a young modernized country, modernization and marketization in China are the product of invasion and shock by capitalist powers, which was initially a passive response, an exogenous change, but was later transformed to be the active response, as the exogenous change promoted and stimulated the endogenous change. Reform is the active response to the external challengers. From the historical perspective, the reform inside is an inevitable outcome of opening up to the outside, and the Reform and Opening Up are essentially consistent.

First, the goal of reform is to establish the market economy, while the market economy is first the product of western civilization. Therefore, opening up to the outside, particularly opening up to the western world, is actually opening up to the developed market economy and introducing in advanced technologies, products, management methods and economic systems from countries of the developed market economy. As a result of compliance with so-called international practices, it necessarily leads to transformation of the domestic economic system based on general rules of the developed market economy and rapid transformation of the domestic economic system to the market economy. The degree of opening up to the outside determines the degree of reform inside. The reform experiences in China have provided a vivid example for this point. The sequence of opening up of Chinese economy from the earliest special economic zones, coastal area, border region, river area, roadside area to inland is generally the same as the sequence of marketization development in different regions, and the sequence of opening up from the commodity market to the capital market is generally the same as the sequence of release of control from the commodity market to the capital market.

Second, the modern market economy is essentially internalized. The market economy aiming at creating value and gaining currency shows the trend of unlimited expansion, which broke the mutually closed status among different nations along with large-scale mechanized industry and free trade and turned the human history into the real "world history". The development of socialized large-scale production and market economy increasingly link all countries and nations together; the domestic market and international market and the national economy and world economy have become an integral part; the commodity market, capital market and labor market become increasingly internalized; and a "modern world system" of all countries and nations has been constructed based on the market economy.

The consistency between Reform and Opening Up enables opening up to the outside to become a basic national policy for construction of the socialism with Chinese characteristics. As pointed out by Deng Xiaoping, the current world is an open world and the development of China is indispensable from the world.

> Opening up to the outside world is of great significance. It is impossible for any country to develop if it is isolated from the world and refuses to strengthen international communication and introduce advanced experiences, technologies and funds from developed countries.

As guided by the spirit, China expands opening up from the economic sector to the technology, education and culture area, and from the coastal area to the border, riverside and inland area, boldly introduces things from the outside, then goes out of the country and realizes the comprehensive development of opening-up undertakings of China.

Reform and Opening Up are consistent with each other while also shows an inherent contradiction, which still results from the special goal of reform in China. Generally, the modern world system is a capitalist world system made up by center countries, semi-periphery countries and periphery countries, where the capitalist economic relations and political order play the deciding role, and the capitalist economic rules dominate the world market and international economic relations. It means that the market economy is not neutral, at least in the world range. As we consider that the market economy is worldwide and the world economic order is capitalist, the practical socialist system is essentially national, while it can only survive and develop when it maintains relative independence from the worldwide capitalist order. Karl Marx and Friedrich Engels once believed that the socialist revolution could only succeed when it broke out in several major capitalist countries simultaneously and constituted a worldwide phenomenon. However, the socialism was practically established in relatively backward countries and showed closer relation to the nationalism. Vladimir Lenin's theory of the socialist revolution in one nation, Joseph Stalin's theory on the construction of socialism in one nation, Mao Zedong's theories of new democracy and various kinds of socialist ideas in the third world countries all reflected nationalism.

The socialism as a national phenomenon and the market system as the world phenomenon present a complicated relationship of mutual connection, mutual dependence, mutual segmentation and mutual contradiction. By opening up and actively participating in international labor division and international competition, it facilitates domestic reform and development and accelerates the process of modernization, but meanwhile makes domestic economy, politics and culture rely on and be restricted by the international capitalist order more. Therefore, in order to guarantee the relative stability of the socialist constitutional system, it is necessary to maintain independence and autonomy while actively promoting opening up, so the Opening Up of China must be gradual and conditional. It is also a basic national policy of China to correctly deal with the relation between opening up and autonomy and correctly treat the modern civilization results created by the capitalist society. According to this national policy, as the commonwealth of the human society, we shall boldly learn and draw experiences from the advanced material civilization and spiritual civilization created by developed capitalist countries in economic, political, scientific and technological, education, cultural and management sector, and, on the other hand, as opening up also brings in some corruptive and negative things of the capitalism, when studying the advanced experiences of the capitalism, we shall adhere to the policy of independence and self-reliance and focus on relying on our own strength, combine introduction with opening up and innovation and combine use of foreign funds and our own accumulations, and thus realize the healthier development of opening up. The perfect combination of independence and Reform and Opening Up renders another important institutional guarantee for the gradual reform in China.

XI. Economic reform and political reform

The starting point for the radical reform is the "opening" and diversity of politics. The western-style political structure of political diversity or multiparty system constitutes the political foundation for the radical reform, which fundamentally damages the socialist constitutional system and the original economic and political order and leads to irreversible profound change of the economic system. According to western mainstream economists and politicians, the diversity of the political system is the necessary political prerequisite for the market economy and the economic reform in China will be destined to be stuck in trouble due to lack of the prerequisite. Another popular saying is that the characteristic of reform in China lies in that China will carry out economic reform first and political reform next, with the economic reform ahead of the political reform. It does not conform to reality.

As a matter of fact, along with the transition from the planned economy to the market economy, the political structure and political system in China have also been exposed to important and profound changes, mainly shown in the following aspects:

- Political democracy. Since the 3rd Plenary Session of the 11th Central Committee, the construction of the socialist democracy and the legal system has ushered in great development. The democratic centralism within the Party has been restored, the system of people's congress has been completed, the system of division of powers of the national authority has been improved and the citizens' political rights have been expanded.
- Construction of legal system. The complete socialist legal system has been built and constantly improved, providing reliable guarantee for the democratic national political system and citizens' democratic rights.
- Separation of the Party and politics. The Party of Communist is the political and policy leader and shall behave in the scope of the Constitution and laws. The confirmation on this system creates conditions for carrying forward the socialist democracy and giving full play to the role of government.
- Separation of government and enterprises. The separation of government and enterprises help enterprises get rid of the administrative dependence of the government, which fundamentally breaks the highly concentrated traditional economic and political system and changes the situation of unity of politics and economy into one.
- Administrative decentralization. Decentralization has widely developed, governments at all levels are more clear about their independent power, interests and performance goals and the new pattern of the relation between the central government and local government has emerged.
- Social stratification. Along with deepening economic reform, differences between different areas, different sectors, different industries and different social ranks are increasingly evident, and the class and rank structure of Chinese society and the corresponding ideas are increasingly differentiated, etc.

Though without a grand and spectacular scale, all these changes are happening profoundly in a long run, which are the product of the changes to the economic system as well as the prerequisite for changes to the economic system.

However, the political reform in China and the radical reform in the Soviet Union and Eastern Europe contain different meanings. In terms of the goal, the reform of the political system in China regards the socialist democracy as the goal, which is under the framework of the socialist constitutional system. The essence of the socialist democracy is people being the master, mainly realized by the system of people's congress. Major measurement criteria include whether the state leadership can be orderly replaced according to laws, whether all people can manage state affairs and social affairs as well as economic and cultural undertakings according to laws, whether the masses can smoothly express their interest requirements, whether all circles of the society can effectively join in the political life of the state, whether state decisions are scientific and democratic, whether talents from all circles can join the state leadership and management system through fair competition, whether the ruling party can lead the state affairs according to the Constitution and laws and whether application of authority is subject to effective restraint and supervision.[20] Regarding the priority of reform, the Reform in China takes economic construction as the central task. The main meaning of taking economic construction as the central task is as follows:

(1) For the part of the political system reform that is directly integrated with the economic system, such as narrowing the scope of direct intervention by the government, separating politics from the economy, separating government from enterprises and separating the responsibilities as the government and as the state-owned assets manager, delegating power to the lower levels and transformation of functions and establishment of the indirect control system, the simultaneous reform shall be implemented according to demands on economic reform.

(2) For the part of the political system reform involved as the necessary condition for success of the economic reform measures, such as democratic and scientific decision making, legal system, structural establishment, reform of the personnel system relating to cadres and construction of the Party's working style and clean government, it shall be promoted along with or even properly ahead of economic reform.

(3) For the part of the political system reform that is restricted by the level of economic reform and economic development but meanwhile is of great significance to the political system and political stability, such as expansion of political participation, reform of the electoral system and development of social self-governance, the progress shall not be too fast or too slow, but shall be steadily promoted along with deepening economic reform and gradual mature objective conditions.

(4) For the part of the political system reform that is of greater independence and exerts favorable influence on economic reform and economic development, such

as improving the democratic centralism within the Party, the supervision and restraint on the government power and the people's congress, it shall be actively carried out based on demands of the political system reform itself.

(5) The political system reform shall create a favorable social environment for economic reform and economic development and shall favor the stability of politics and social order, which means to temporarily control the measures of political reform that are theoretically rational but may practically affect political stability and thus damage economic reform and economic development.[21]

This special strategy of the political reform is the necessary requirement by the essence of the gradual reform as well as the necessary condition for the balance between the industrialization, marketization and the socialist constitutional system, and plays a positive role in successfully carrying out the gradual reform:

(1) During the transition to the market economy, various unstable factors have significantly increased along with violent changes of the social structure and increasingly fierce conflict between the new and the old systems. The relative political stability and concentration is favorable to preventing the society from losing control, excluding interference by political turmoil to economic construction, reducing the damage and loss incurred by the conflict between the new and the old systems in the Reform, concentrating on economic construction and creating a normal social environment for reform and development.

(2) Being the fundamental adjustment to the existing interest structure, reform may bring about various conflicts in interests. An extremely high cost would result if these conflicts were settled through negotiation or currency exchange. The gradual reform makes full use of the political authority of the Party and government formed during long-term revolution and construction,[22] resolves conflicts through mobilization, compulsion and political guide by the government, lowers the cost of reform and reduces the reform resistance.

(3) The direction and steps of the political system reform shall be decided according to requirements of economic reform and economic development, which is favorable to economic development and complies with laws of political development. Based only on the constant progress of the productive forces and the constant improvement of the economic system, the mature socialist democratic politics and favorable political order can be gradually established. If compulsorily implementing a certain mode of political system without certain economic foundation, it would necessarily lead to huge damage to productive forces.

In the socialist system, due to the mainstay position of the public ownership and the leading role of the government, the bond between the economy and politics is tighter than ever. How to correctly treat the relation between economy and politics and between the political reform and economic reform is now of special significance. Against this issue, the gradual reform in China has acquired unique experiences and is meanwhile faced with great challenges.

XII. Role of initial conditions

When explaining the causes for the emergence of different roads, the gradual reform in China and the radical reform in the former Soviet Union and Eastern European countries, a large number of scholars think highly of the role of initial conditions. For example, Jeffrey Sachs et al. concluded the favorable initial conditions for reform in China as the backward economic structure, and Qian Yingyi et al. believed that the success of reform in China mainly benefited from the M structure of the traditional system – i.e., the "block-block" structure of multiple layers and regions based on the regional principle (i.e., M economy). In the M organization, the grassroots government has greater autonomy, and the relation between regions is horizontal and market-oriented. This structure weakens the administrative control, strengthens market activities and stimulates the development of non-state-owned enterprises.[23] The *Role of Reform and Planning in the 1990s*, the investigation report on Chinese economy by the WB, once afforded much food for thought and concluded the favorable initial conditions for Chinese reform as the lagging return of materials investment before the Reform. For example, infrastructure for agriculture including materials, sales and labors has been established during the period of People's Commune, but the incentive factor was lacked in agriculture. Once the personal incentive measure was introduced and the role of the government was reformed, the rapid development of output would be foreseen. For another example, the industrialization has been significantly improved after 1949, particularly the heavy industry and big and medium-sized state-owned enterprises. On the one hand, it meant that China had already the basis for construction of industry of a large scale, and, on the other hand, after the investment was lowered to people, many investment opportunities in the light industry could be found.[24]

Some other favorable conditions often mentioned include:

- The level of the planned economy in China before reform was low, the system was dispersed inside and the traditional planned economy was severely damaged in the ten-year "Great Cultural Revolution". However, in the Soviet Union and Eastern European countries, the organization of the planned economy is relatively strict.
- Compared to the Soviet Union and Eastern European countries, the Reform in China had one special favorable condition – i.e., the support by numerous overseas Chinese and the Chinese economic circle. They were not only the intermediary for opening up but also fund provider. The great amount of funds from Chinese overseas constantly flew from overseas to China, playing an active role in promoting Reform and Opening Up and economic development.

- The Reform in China was carried out under the background of non-severe economic and political crisis and did not need the shock treatment and radical reform. However, the radical reform of the Soviet Union and Eastern European countries was conducted under constant economic stagnation, increasingly intensified inflation and severe political crisis.
- In the Soviet Union and Eastern European countries, the crisis in the social security system had become an important factor inhibiting economic growth during the transition. They had to contribute a large proportion of the national income to social security to maintain social stability, which was unfavorable to economic growth. However, in China, the social security system was still based on the traditional big family, so the cost in this area was not too high and the proportion of the social security in the budget expenditure was very low. This is a very favorable factor for economic growth.[25]

Though the division between the gradual reform and radical reform has a considerable relation to differences of initial conditions, but it is not convincing to merely attribute the generation of the two different roads to differences of initial conditions. As a matter of fact, though the Soviet Union and China had many differences in the economic system, economic structure and cultural traditions, it was undeniable that the two countries also shared many things in common. After all, both countries had once applied the highly concentrated planned economic system, the development strategy of giving priority to heavy industry and the ideology of collectivism. More importantly, reform is a self-conscious social action, the process of "public choice" by different social groups. For reformers, advantages and disadvantages of initial conditions are only relative, and people have no choice. The key is how to understand and make use of these conditions and make the correct choice that complies with practices. The favorable initial conditions do not necessarily lead to the success of the Reform, while the unfavorable initial conditions do not necessarily lead to failure of the Reform. There is no direct and decisive correspondence between initial conditions and reform results. Jeffrey Sachs et al. believed that the economic structure of the Soviet Union determined that the gradual reform was unavailable there, but the "shock treatment" and "Big Bang" were the only choice. This idea completely excluded social choice and people's activities, and it was not convincing. People actually acquire totally different conclusions from different perspectives regarding the influence of the initial economic structure. For example, according to Roy Medvedev, the initial conditions of Russia decided that it was unable to rapidly develop the modern capitalist system because of many severe obstacles on the road of capitalist development of Russia, including (1) the strength of materials – i.e., the rigid traditional system; (2) role of the legacy of the Cold War and military complex; (3) geology, nature and economy of Russia; (4) the spirit of "enterprise operation" and Russian spirit; (5) increasing resistance by people; (6) complexity of the market mechanism; (7) the structural reform demanding both time and capital; (8) competition by western countries; (9) lack of state ideas and ideology of the radical reform; and (10) weak and vague motive force for capitalist revolution.[26] These factors demanded the gradual reform instead of the radical reform. People's choice and the corresponding responsibilities shall not be ignored with objective conditions as the excuse during historical development and transition. As a matter of fact, Mikhail Gorbachev must bear the responsibility for the failure of the gradual reform in the Soviet Union and the emergence of the "Big Bang" strategy. In 1985 when he assumed the power, he did not bring any new thing to the Reform but proposed the "acceleration strategy" that completely repeated the old road of the planned economy and finally led to excessive investment and budget deficit. In 1986, the 27th Congress of the Communist Party of the Soviet Union proposed the policy of "fundamental reform" and formulated the corresponding reform plan. However, these reforms were conducted on the basis of the basic state-owned ownership and did not go beyond the framework of "planned economy containing the market mechanism", so delegating powers to lower levels resulted in short-term enterprise behaviors and imbalance of the macro-economy, which finally failed. To overcome the crisis, Mikhail Gorbachev turned to the political "openness", which intensified various economic and political conflicts, pushed the economy and society into difficulties and lost the last opportunity for reform.

Therefore, different reform roads are the products of initial conditions, the results of people's practices, choices and creations, different policies and guide-lines, and results of common action of the leading group and all people in the historical process of reform.

XIII.   Summary: why China leads the road of the gradual reform

As indicated by the earlier analysis, the choice between the gradual reform and the radical reform is not decided by people's subjective preference, but the essence, goal and guiding ideology of the economic system reform. Following causes deter-mine that China leads the road of the gradual reform instead of the radical reform.

First, the Reform in China improves and develops the socialist system instead of fundamentally denying the socialist system, and therefore necessarily emphasizes on the continuity, stability and compatibility of reform in terms of choosing the road of the institutional transition, refuses to scrap it and start all over again and opposes history nihilism. The new system and the old system here are not clearly divided or contradicted since the beginning, but show evident continuity and suc-cession. The transition between them needs to experience many different stages and many intermediate links and apply many intermediate forms. Meanwhile, it is an unprecedented undertaking to combine the basic socialist system with the market economy and develop the market economy under the socialist conditions, which must go through a long-term, complicated historical process from estab-lishment, perfection to maturity and could never be accomplished at one stroke. People's understandings about the socialist market economy are constantly enrich-ing and developing through practices. It fundamentally decides that the economic reform in China could not choose the radical reform applied by the Soviet Union and Eastern European countries previously. In this way, China has maintained the stable and constant development through the process of economic reform and avoided the disastrous consequences of the radical reform.

Second, though the establishment of the market economic system demands the scientific strategic planning and specific implementation proposal and shall be carried out as planned, the transition of the social system is different for the construction of roads or houses on earth, where an elaborate and detailed construction drawing must be provided in advance, and the fixed process must be abided by. The social and economic form, particularly the form of the market economy, is a complicated organic system, and the spontaneous law of value is adjusting the whole economic life. Correspondingly, the generation and development of the market economy also show the feature of spontaneous evolution to a certain degree but is not completely decided by people's subjective will and pre-design. This is an important reason for emphasis on trials. Through all these trials, the laws are gradually understood, and the truth is gradually unveiled. From this perspective, in the process of reform deepening, it is necessary to adhere to respecting people's initiative, give full play to the initiative, enthusiasm and creativity of the grassroots units, carry out reform under the Party's leadership and perfectly combine trials in practices and strengthening of the top design.

Third, as the adjustment to the production relations, essentially the adjustment to the interest relations, the Reform aims to mobilize the initiative and enthusiasm of all aspects, guarantee interests of all parties and promote the development of the productive forces. In this sense, Reform and Opening Up is the undertaking of billions of people, so people's initiative must be respected. However, in China, such a big country of vast land and complicated conditions, interests of all parties are extremely complicated and diverse, including the interests between the urban and rural area, between different regions, between China and foreign countries, between the central and local government, between individuals and collectives, between the part and the whole and between the current and long-term interests. Therefore, it requires us adhering to principles, making an overall design, considering all different factors, systematically carrying out reform, respecting interests and requests of all parties, encouraging explorations and tests, tolerating diversity, reflecting opinions of all parties, mobilizing initiative of all parties and preventing rigid uniformity during reform.

Fourth, the Reform aims to better liberate and develop productive forces, improve people's welfare, promote all-around development of people and realize common prosperity of the society. This shall be the criterion for judgment on success or failure of the Reform and shall be tested by results of practices. The test also demands a long-term process of exchange, comparison and repetition, which is the basic principle of dialectical materialism and historical materialism. If designing the Reform proposal merely based on theoretical theories and principles without the foundation of certain practical experiences and process and carrying out measures of drastic reform from top to bottom, it would easily make the mistake of dogmatism and finally result in the ideology and methodology leading to the failure of the radical reform. The gradual reform in China adheres to emancipating the mind, seeking truth from facts and proceeding from reality, testing the success and failure of the Reform with the criteria of whether it is favorable to developing productive forces in the socialist society, whether it is favorable to promoting the comprehensive strength of the socialist country and whether it is favorable to improving people's living standards. In this way, it acquires the magic key to success from the world outlook and methodology.

As proved by practices, the gradual reform in China is a successful way of reform. Then, shall the gradual reform be further applied when deepening the economic system reform under new historical conditions? The answer is yes. The choice for the economic reform in China to apply the gradual reform method is fundamentally determined by the special essence of the goal of the socialist market economy, so it will not vary along with changes to domestic and foreign economic conditions. However, it shall be noted that, compared with previous economic reform, the conditions and tasks of Chinese economic reform at the current stage have been exposed to some important changes, so the specific method of reform will necessarily change. First, as the economic system has been increasingly matured, people's understandings about laws of reform have been constantly deepening, which requires paying more attention to overall design, overall arrangements and systematic implementation when deepening reform. Second, as the economic interests become increasingly diversified and social conflicts become increasingly complicated, people's divergence and dispute on understandings of the Reform will be intensified, which requires taking all factors into consideration, widely building consensus and forming the joint forces for reform when deepening the Reform. Third, as the socialist market economic system is gradually improved, the dual-track system of the incremental and storage reform and the new system and the old system have smaller space for existence, which requires paying more attention to the storage reform and forming the universal market system. Fourth, as the major tasks of the economic system reform are gradually completed, the Reform of the society and people's living standard becomes more important, which requires paying more attention to justice and equity when deepening reform.

Notes

1 Refer to Ha-Joon and Peter Nolan, *The Transformation of the Communist Economies*, Mst. Mrtin's Press, 1995, Page 401–402.
2 [Belgium] Gerard Roland, *Transition and Economics*, translated by Zhang Fan et al., Peking University Press, Edition 2002.
3 According to the quantitative comparison between authentic GDP data from 1988 to 2012 of the United Nations Statistical Office, in the past 24 years (22 years for Russia and Ukraine), the annual average GDP growth rates of major countries and regions are listed in sequence as follows: China (9.7), Latin America (6.7), India (6.4), East Asia (3.8), Poland (2.9), world average (2.8); America (2.5), Germany and Western Europe (1.8), Japan (1.3), Eastern Europe (1.0), Hungary (0.8), Russia (0.6) and Ukraine (−1.6). Only Poland out of transitional countries in Eastern Europe is slightly higher than the world average level. If comparing the ratio of economic growth within 24 years, China is 930%, the world is 179%, America is 183%, Western Europe is 153%, Eastern Europe is 128%, Hungary is 120%, Russia is 116% and Ukraine has only 70% of the year 1990. Refer to Chen Ping, "From Liberalism to Neo-conservatism – Comment on

Janos Kornai's Be Vigilant Against the Immediate Threat", *Observer* [Online], August 11, 2014.

4 Lin Yifu, Cai Fang, and Li Zhou, *Chinese Miracle: Development Strategy and Economic Reform* (enlarged edition), Truth & Wisdom Press, Shanghai Joint Publishing, Shanghai People's Publishing House, Edition 2014.

5 [US] Joseph E. Stigliz, *Where Is the Reform Leading? – On Transition in the Decade*, referring to Hu An'gang and Wang Shaoguang, *Government and Market*, China Planning Press, Edition 2000.

6 [US] Elinor Ostrom et al., *Institutional Analysis and Reflection on Development*, translated by Wang Cheng et al., The Commercial Press, Edition 1996.

7 Zhou Zhenhua, *System Reform and Economic Growth – Analysis of Chinese Experiences and Model*, Shanghai Joint Publishing, Shanghai People's Publishing House, Edition 1999.

8 János Kornai, *Highway and Byways*, MIT Press, 1995. Though Janos Kornai et al. recognized the key role of the constitutional system, we disagree with their opinions. First, they firmly define the essence and goal of economic transformation as the transition from socialism to capitalism and their so-called constitutionalism is the capitalist constitutional system, which fundamentally denies the possibility of the socialist market economy and basic experiences of the gradual reform in China. Second, they emphasize the significance of the constitutionalism in a one-sided way, regard the constitutionalism as a kind of transcendental fixed thing, replace the rational goal of marketization and resources allocation with the goal of transition of the constitutionalism and ignore the dynamic evolution relation between the institutional arrangement and constitutional system of mutual effect, penetration and interaction.

9 Lin Yifu, "Theories on Economics on Institutional Changes: Induced Changes and Compulsory Changes", *Cato Journal*, Cato Institute, Washington DC, Vol. 9, 1989, Page 1–33.

10 Kornai, *Highway and Byways*, MIT Press, 1995.

11 Though privatization is an economic issue, we shall first consider it as a political concept in the transition economy – i.e., the transition process from the economy with the public ownership as the main body to the economy with the private ownership as the main body. We shall not call the establishment of a private enterprise or the transfer from a state-owned enterprise to a private enterprise as privatization and shall not call the establishment of a state-owned enterprise or the transfer from a private enterprise to a state-owned enterprise as socialism. The essence of the transition economy can only be mastered when the concept of privatization is understood. For example, the proportion of the non-state-owned economy in China is currently similar to Russia, but the institutional structure of the two countries show great differences due to different constitutional systems. China adheres to the public ownership as the main body, while Russia is making the private economy the foundation of its whole economic system and political system. Privatization first refers to the dynamic process of reform of the whole economic and political system on the basis of private ownership. Of course, the relation between the quantitative and qualitative change shall be considered here, as the accumulation of quantitative changes to a certain degree transforms to the qualitative change.

12 Olivier Blanchard and Richard Layard, *How to Privatize, the Transformation of Socialist Economies*, edited by Hores Siebers, J·C·B·Mohr Tubingen, 1992.

13 [US], Jean C. Oi, "Fiscal Reform and the Economic Foundation of Local State Corporatism in China", *World Politics*, Vol. 45, 1992, 1st Issue, Page 99–126.

14 Cao Yuan Zhang, Ying Yi Qian, and Barry R. Weingast, "From Federalism, Chinese Style, to Privatzation, Chinese Style", *Economics of Transition*, Vol. 7, 1999, Page 103–131.

15 Yang Ruilong, "Three Stages for System Transition Methods in China", Economic Research, 1998, 1st Issue, Page 5-12.

16   Shen Liren and Dai Yuanchen, "Generation of 'Duke Economy' in China and Its Weaknesses and Sources", *Economic Research Journal*, 1990, 3rd Issue, Page 1–19, 67.

17   Wang Shaoguang and Hu An'gang, *Report on the State Capacity of China*, refer to Dong Fureng, *Centralization and Decentralization – Construction of the Relation Between the Central and Local Government*, Economic Science Press, Edition 1996.

18   Olivier Blanchard and Andrei Shleifer, "Federalism With and Without Political Centralization: China Versus Russia", Working Paper, 2000, www.nber.org/papers/w7616

19   Luo Rongqu, *New Theories on Modernization*, Peking University Press, Edition 1993.

20   Xi Jinping, "Speech on the Celebration Meeting for the 60th Anniversary of Foundation of the National People's Congress", *People's Daily*, September 5, 2004.

21   Guo Shuqing, *Reform of Model and Model of Reform*, Shanghai Joint Publishing Press, Edition 1989, Page 276–277.

22   "Authority is a kind of special organizational resource. The application of authority needs no cost, as the authority may be conferred upon before it plays the role, lasts stable and long and incorporates a large behavior category. When a response is requested then, the authority often requires no remuneration, punishment, control and even persuasion". [US] Charles E. Lindblom, *Politics and Market*, translated by Wang Yizhou, Shanghai Joint Publishing Press, Edition 1992, Page 22.

23   Qian Yingyi and Xu Chenggang, "Why the Economic Reform Is Different From Others", *Economic and Social System Comparison*, 1993, 10th Issue, Page 29–40.

24   World Bank, *Role of Reform and Planning in the 1990s*, China Financial and Economic Publishing House, Edition 1993, Page 4.

25   László Csaba, "The Political Economy of the Reform Strategy: China and Eastern Europe Compared", *Communist & Economic Transformation*, Vol. 8, 1st Issue, 1996, Page 53–65.

26   [Russia] Roy Medvedev, *Where Is Russia Leading to*, translated by Guan Guihai and Wang Xiaoyu, The Contemporary World Press, Edition 2003.

5 Market failure does not constitute the basis for existence of the state-owned economy – concurrently on the status and role of the state-owned economy in the socialist market economy

How to correctly understand the status and role of state-owned economy in the socialist market economy is a fundamental issue concerning the essence and development direction of our society and the prospect, fate and reform of China. However, some one-sided and even wrong understandings on this issue which are currently popular need to be clarified, including a representative idea that attributes the basis for existence of the state-owned economy to market failure and non-competitiveness. Some people believe that the existence of the state-owned economy is limited to the scope of "market failure", and the goal of reform of the state-owned economy is to pull the state-owned economy out of competitive industries and make it dedicated to the sector of public goods and natural monopoly where private enterprises are not willing to run businesses due to "market failure" or the market mechanism cannot play its adjusting role, thus to complement the deficiency of private enterprises and the market mechanism. This opinion that regards the function and role of the state-owned economy as "complementing the market failure" is theoretically and practically untenable and is extremely misleading in practices. We shall have a clear understanding about it.

I. The theory attributing the basis for existence of the state-owned economy to a complement to "market failure" does not accord with the practical conditions of development of state-owned economies in different countries

In the socialist countries adopting the planned economy, the state-owned economy occupies an absolutely dominating position in the national economy, so its scope of existence is non-related to the so-called market failure. Even in countries with developed capitalist market economies, the distribution of the state-owned economy is not restricted to the sector of "market failure" providing public commodities and natural monopoly. After the Second World War, developed capitalist countries have been exposed to several waves of nationalization and have established a large number of state-owned enterprises, involving petroleum, coal, electricity, iron and steel, railway, highway, port, civil aviation, electronics, astronavigation, automobile, airplane, bank, insurance and public services, etc. (see Table 5.1).

Table 5.1 Distribution of State-Owned Enterprises in Key Departments in Major Capitalist Countries in 1978

	Post	Telecom	Power	Gas	Petroleum	Coal	Railway	Aviation	Iron and Steel	Automobile	Ship Building
UK	■	■	■	■	▼	■	■	◆	◆	■	■
Italy	■	■	◆	■	NA	NA	■	■	▼	◆	◆
France	■	■	■	■	NA	■	■	◆	◆	■	□
West Germany	■	■	◆	■	▼	■	■	■	▼	□	▼
Japan	■	■	□	□	NA	□	■	▼	□	□	□
South Korea	■	■	◆	□	NA	▼	◆	□	◆	□	□
Canada	■	▼	■	□	□	□	■	◆	□	□	□
Austria	■	■	■	■	■	■	■	■	■	■	NA
Spain	■	■	□	◆	NA	■	■	■	□	□	◆
Australia	■	■	■	■	NA	NA	■	■	□	□	NA
Sweden	■	■	▮	■	NA		■	◆	□	□	◆
America	■	□	□	□	□	□	▼	□	□	□	□

Source: *Harvard Business Review*, March–April 1979, page 161

Note: ■ approximate to 100% state-owned, ◆: 75% state-owned, ▮: 50% state-owned, ▼: 25% state-owned, □: approximate to 100% private owned

In 1979, the turnover of state-owned enterprises in the UK accounted for 11.5% of gross domestic product (GDP) of UK, while the investment amount took up 20%, and in 1982, 53% of companies in France were controlled by the government. The nationalization of the Federal Germany, Austria and Italy had been significantly improved, and the state-owned economy had held the dominant position in many key economic departments.

The state-owned economy is more widely distributed and plays a more important role in developing countries (see Table 5.2).

As shown in the earlier two tables, in the 1970s, the state-owned economy in major capitalist countries not only accounted for a high proportion in industries of public commodities and natural monopoly, such as the post, electricity, telecommunication and gas, but also played a very important role in key competitive markets including coal, petroleum, aviation, iron and steel, automobile and ship making. In developing countries, the state-owned economy was more widely distributed, covering the industries of public commodities and natural monopoly such as electricity, gas and running water, as well as general industries including the commerce, service, architecture and manufacturing, etc. The major goal for capitalist countries to establish these state-owned enterprises was not pursuing maximum profits, but overcoming defects of the private ownership, completing the social goal that private enterprises were not willing or not capable to effectively complete under conditions at that time, guaranteeing conditions for reproduction of capitalist countries and promoting development of the capitalist economy. However, it does not necessarily mean that these state-owned enterprises could not make profits, because, different from ordinary financial expenditure, the capital invested on state-owned enterprises needs to be maintained and appreciated during operation and constantly circulated within the social system of reproduction. In this way, these enterprises could survive and develop in the market economy, effectively complete their social functions and complete the social goal. In this sense, the pursuit of profits and realization of the social goal run parallel without contradiction. Therefore, the "market failure" does not constitute the basis for existence of the state-owned economy.

II. There is no necessary connection between the "market failure" and state-owned economy. The logic attributing the basis for existence of the state-owned economy to the complement to "market failure" necessarily leads to fundamental privatization

The western mainstream economic theories attribute the basis for existence of the state-owned economy to the complement to "market failure" and hold that the state-owned economy is only needed in the area of "market failure" such as the natural monopoly and public commodities. However, according to results of the recent development of the western mainstream economics, there is no necessary connection between the "market failure" and the state-owned economy – i.e., the market failure does not lead to the conclusion of establishment of the state-owned

Table 5.2 Distribution of State-Owned Enterprises in Some Developing Countries Unit: %

Area	Country	Year	Agriculture	Commerce and service	Architecture	Manufacturing	Mining	Traffic and communication	Electricity, gas and running water
Asia	Bangladesh	1980		<25	<25	<25	<25	>50	>75
	Burma	1980		<50	<75	<75	>75	<50	>75
	India	1978				<25	>75	<50	>75
	Pakistan	1980		<25	<25	<25	<25	<50	>75
	South Korea	1974–1977				<25	<25	<50	>75
Africa	Congo	1980			<25	<25	<5	<50	>75
	Kenya	1980				<25	<5	<50	>75
	Tanzania	1980–1981		<50	<25	<50	>75	<25	>75
	Tunisia	1976				<50	<50	<75	>75
Latin America	Argentina	1980				<25	<50	<50	<75
	Uruguay	1980		<5	<5	<5	<5	<25	>75
	Mexico	1979	<25		<5	<5	>75	<75	>75
	Nicaragua	1980	<5	<25	<75	>25	>75	<75	<75

Note: Prepared based on relevant data in *1983 World Economic Report* of the WB

economy. The contemporary economics of regulation believe that the industry of natural monopoly does not necessarily require state-owned enterprises, and natural privatization of the industries of natural monopoly can be realized by operation of private enterprises and control by government on the price, quality and investment. Meanwhile, public commodities can also be provided by private departments. It guarantees effective supply of public commodities and improves the efficiency of supply by private departments and the market supplying the public commodities and government rendering subsidies and supervision. Therefore, even according to the western mainstream economics, the "market failure" does not demand the state-owned economy as the complement, and no necessary causality exists between the two. So, the theory attributing the "market failure" to the basis for existence of the state-owned economy shows conflicts with western mainstream economic theory itself in terms of logic and is not valid.

It shall also be noted that theory that restricts the function of the state-owned economy to the area of "complement to the market failure" and determines the "progress and regression" of reform of the state-owned economy and the so-called good policy on the basis is essentially not the argument on the cause for existence of the state-owned economy, but the argument on restricting and even cancelling the state-owned economy, which theoretically hides great danger. According to western mainstream economists, the market is "omnipotent" as an "invisible hand", while the so-called market failure previously discovered actually does not exist at all and can be solved through the market method under some conditions. Therefore, a direct conclusion can be reached that as the "market failure" does not exist, and the state-owned economy loses its only basis for existence. For example, in the area of natural monopoly, the theory of industrial organization on the dynamic boundary of the natural monopoly increasingly narrows the scope of existence of the natural monopoly. This theory argues that, on the one hand, the original understanding about industries of natural monopoly was inaccurate and many industries considered as natural monopoly actually show no attribute of natural monopoly or have only a part of businesses showing natural monopoly. For example, in the railway sector, the railway network is of natural monopoly, but the passenger and freight transportation on railway can be exposed to competition. On the other hand, along with technical progress and expanding market, the original industries of natural monopoly can be turned into the competitive industries, the technical progress weakens the attribute of natural monopoly of some industries and strengthens the competition, and the expanding market narrows the boundary of the natural monopoly. Therefore, many state-owned enterprises that have existed due to the natural monopoly have no basis for existence now and become the primary goal of privatization. The process of privatization of many countries including America and UK was synchronous with the release of control of industry regulation. For another example, as demonstrated by Coase theorem, the clear ownership interiorizes the external effect of transactions, so the public commodities can be provided by private departments under the market mechanism. For another example, the School of Public Choice proposes the concept of "government failure" and believes that though it may not be the optimum choice to supply public commodities through the market method, it may be more efficient than the supply by the government – i.e., the state-owned enterprises, because the issue of "government failure" is more serious than the "market failure".

In this way, according to the western mainstream economic theories, the state-owned economy not only survives in the narrow area subject to "market failure" but also may increasingly lose its reason for existence along with technical progress, clearer definition of the ownership and improvement of the control method. They believe that the state-owned economy shall wholly exit the competitive area and even shall be privatized in the sector of public commodities and natural monopoly, thus to realize improvement of the overall economic efficiency. It can be seen that the theory of "market failure" that argues the reason for existence of the state-owned enterprises cannot fully present the role of the state-owned economy and hides the theoretical orientation of overall privatization.

III.   The theory attributing the basis for existence of the state-owned economy to a complement to "market failure" ignores the macro-function of the state-owned economy and lacks sufficient basis in terms of micro-efficiency

The western mainstream economic theories believe that the state-owned economy can only exist in the area of "market failure" and is unnecessary and impossible in the broad competitive areas. From the perspective of comparison of the micro-efficiency, they believe that the state-owned economy presents a lower efficiency than the private economy, so the state-owned economy is only needed in the market where private economies are not willing to join or the competition is invalid. Therefore, the fewer state-owned economies would be better and they shall only be applied to public undertakings and industries of ineffective competition, while state-owned enterprises of other industries shall be privatized for the improvement of efficiency. However, the aforementioned theory is a belief of liberalism rather than a science based on facts. The proofs on low efficiency of state-owned enterprises such as the "agency problem", "free ride in company governance" and "soft budget restraint" do not only exist in state-owned enterprises, but are the common issues encountered by all modern joint stock of separated ownership and control power.[1] Moreover, according to numerous empirical researches on comparison of the efficiency of state-owned enterprises and that of private enterprises, there is no final conclusion of efficiency of private enterprises higher than efficiency of state-owned enterprises. In fact, there are some private enterprises of low efficiency and some state-owned enterprises of higher efficiency. Therefore, some scholars summarized that "the private enterprises do not show higher efficiency than public enterprises in the mass" and "in many industries, public ownership and private ownership may share the same efficiency".[2]

It shall be also pointed out that the comparison of the micro-efficiency does not constitute the full reason for agreeing or opposing the state-owned economy. As a form where the state or the social whole occupying the means of production, in addition to realizing the micro-efficiency, the state-owned economy presents a more significant value in its macro-functions. As a matter of fact, the state-owned economies in different countries are bearing the function for the state or the government to intervene in or control on economy to different degrees. On the one hand, the state-owned economy plays the role of "stabilizer" in economy, as pointed out by Tinbergen (1986), "The existence of current investment on public sectors in a certain scale makes very favorable foundation for application of economic counter-cyclical policies", and, on the other hand, the state-owned economy is capable of "making decisions with the long-term development as the goals, which are not or may not be the decisions favoring maximum profits" (Kaldor, 1980), thus to guarantee long-term dynamic balance of the national economy. Moreover, the state-owned economy also plays an important role in realizing equal distribution. For example, the state-owned enterprises could lower the price of life necessities of low-income earners and thus influence on the true distribution of the national income (Bos, 1986); besides, state-owned enterprises also help guarantee equality among citizens within the region and ensure that residents living in remote areas could enjoy some important social services (Zhang Xiazhun, 2007). Therefore, the macro-functions of the state-owned economies have been ignored if only arguing the basis for existence of state-owned economies from the perspective of micro-efficiency.

Fundamentally speaking, the goal of establishment of the state-owned economy is not to improve the private efficiency from the micro-level. In addition to the partial failure at the micro-level, the more severe defect of the market mechanism lies in that it fails to guarantee the long-term dynamic balance of the national economy, so the overall planned control from the social level is demanded. Classic writers of Marxism based on the basic conflicts between the socialization of production and the capitalist private ownership of means of production and reached conclusion that means of production shall be occupied by the society. The most effective measure to realize the macro-control of the state is indispensable from direct adjustment to the process of economic operation and maintains the control over major industries and key areas related to the lifeline of the national economy, while the state-owned economy makes the economic foundation of the direct control. The structure, direction and proportion of economic development formulated by the state for the long-term development of economy is often inconsistent with the structure, direction and proportion spontaneously formed in the market. The national planned adjustment and macro-control must have its role exceed the market in many aspects and clearly guide the economic development in a long run. Therefore, it shall not only rely on short-term demand policies including fiscal policies and currency policies, but shall be more dependent on supply policies, structure policies and direct adjustment by the government, which can only be enforced based on certain proportion of state-owned economies. Consequently, the state-owned economy is the important foundation and measure for the macro-control by the state. In this way, the state-owned economy exists due to requirements on overcoming market defects. However, it shall be noticed that the market defect mentioned here is different from the market failure. The market failure is a concept in the micro-level, mainly referring to phenomena of externality, public goods, imperfect competition and information asymmetry, while the market defect is a concept in the macro-level, mainly referring to the spontaneity, blindness, hysteresis and injustice of the market. The existence of the state-owned economy is more related to the market defects than merely the market failure. As pointed out by Jiang Zemin,

> To achieve success in establishment of the socialist market economic system, it is necessary to perfectly combine the socialist market economic system with the basic socialist system. Therefore, we shall try to combine advantages of the basic socialist system with advantages of the market, make full use of merits of the market such as being more sensitive to various economic signals, give full play to the fundamental role of market in resources allocation, meanwhile overcome the weaknesses and negative aspects of the market economy such as blindness and spontaneity through macro-control and better reflect the superiority of the socialist system in China.[3]

IV.   The theory attributing the basis for existence of the state-owned economy to a complement to "market failure" only considers the abstract concept of the market economy but fails to consider differences between different social systems and requirements of basic economic system

In western capitalist countries, the generation and development of state-owned economies not only relies on considerations about the market failure but also has a great relation with the political goal and values of these countries at that time. The role of the state-owned economy in realizing the goal of social values has been widely recognized by many countries. The large scale of nationalization in European countries after the World War II was the government intervention applied by these countries to overcome the shortage of raw materials at that time, optimize the structure of industrial production and guarantee necessary social services, meanwhile was also related to the common socialism ideological trend in these countries at that time. The British Labor Party, French Social Democratic Party and other left parties in power at that time all regarded nationalization as the necessary measure to realize social equality and democracy, believed that the expansion of public ownership and public services could change the social pattern of rights distribution, realized the new social and economic balance by restricting private capitals and improving workers' rights and, thus, achieved the "real industrial democracy". For example, the Germany Social Democratic Party described the significance of public ownership in *Goteborg Programme1959* as follows:

> The public ownership is a legal form of public supervision that won't be renounced by any modern country. It could protect freedom from being damaged by dominating big-economic organizations. The control power of big

enterprises is mainly mastered by managers, who actually serve for anony-
mous power. Therefore, in these enterprises, the private ownership of mean
of production has lost its control power to certain degree. The central issue
nowadays is the economic power. In any place where the economic power
relation cannot be established by other measures, the public ownership is
appropriate and necessary.[4]

Gaitskell, the economist of the British Labor Party and the former Chancellor of
the Exchequer of the Labor Party government, once mentioned in the book *Socialism and Nationalization* that

> The nationalization of production, distribution and exchange measures would
> promote equality, facilitate implementation of employment policies, combine
> the power that makes important economic decisions and greater responsibili-
> ties for the state, enable the successful development of industrial democracy
> and reduce the inexorability and conflicts in the economic relations.[5]

In socialist countries, the state-owned economy is directly related to the basic
socialist system or basic characteristics of the socialist system. The socialist system is based on the public ownership of means of production, which is the basic
principle of the scientific socialism as well as essential features of the socialism
with Chinese characteristics. It is one of the basic economic systems at the primary
stage of socialism in China to keep public ownership as the mainstay of the economy and allow diverse forms of ownership to develop side by side. The socialist
market economy combines the market economy with the basic socialist system. It
is the core issue of the socialist market economy to realize the effective combination of the public ownership and the market economy. The fundamental goal for
us to establish and develop the socialist market economy and promote reform of
state-owned enterprises is combine the public ownership with the market economy,
adapt the public-owned enterprises particularly the state-owned enterprises to
market competition and enable them to develop in the market competition. One
important reason and manifestation for success of the economic reform in China
lies in the establishment of the new style of state-owned economy management
system and mechanism that adapts to the market economic system. If state-owned
enterprises could only survive in areas free from competition and should exit areas
of competition, then state-owned economies should not exist; the objective foundation was lost for the state-owned economy to exert the control, influence and
driving force, establishment and improvement of the socialist market economy
became an empty talk; the direction was lost for deepening of reform of state-
owned economy, and the great achievement of reform of state-owned economies in
over three decades since the Reform and Opening Up ended in smoke. According
to practical conditions, in addition to special industries such as the military, power
grid, petroleum and petrochemical industry, as well as telecommunications, state-
owned enterprises in China are mostly exposed to effective competition instead of
all being in monopolized industry and are mostly not monopoly enterprises, such

as the state-owned enterprises in sectors of finance, culture, coal, power, equipment manufacturing, automobile, electronic information, architecture, iron and steel, nonferrous metal, chemical, survey and design and science and technology. Though these industries and sectors are not monopolized, they are of great significance in consolidating the socialist system, realizing the goal of macro-control, safeguarding economic safety of the state, promoting independent innovation, guaranteeing equality and justice and establishing the harmonious labor relationship. From the perspective of global competition, very few state-owned enterprises can be counted as monopolized enterprises. To say the least, if state-owned enterprises exited from areas of competition and became monopolized enterprises, would the criticism and attack to the state-owned economy disappear? In these conditions, someone would jump out and say that monopoly is unnecessary and the monopoly should be broken to release the control over operation. This is exactly the same with the criticism of so-called state-owned monopolized sectors by some people. Therefore, we shall understand that the strategic adjustment to the state-owned economy in China is based on the demands of the development of the socialist market economy instead of monopoly or competition. The reform and development of the state-owned economy does not aim to solve the issue of market failure but aims to solve the issue of "plan failure" and market defect, combine the public ownership with the market economy and give better play to advantages of the market economy and the socialist system. In China, the market failure has no direct logic relation with generation and development of the state-owned economy.

V. The theory attributing the basis for existence of the state-owned economy to a complement to "market failure" only considers the static characteristics of the market economy but fails to consider differences between economic development stages of different countries

The scale and area of the state-owned economy are exposed to dynamic changes instead of being changeless. In different stages of economic development in a country, the existence basis and role of the state-owned economy are not completely the same. Generally speaking, the significance of the state-owned economy is greater in developing countries than in developed countries. In developing countries, private capitals are relatively weaker and private enterprise systems show relatively greater defects, and private capitals are often not willing or capable to invest on energy, traffic and infrastructure, etc., necessary for economic development as they are not profit-oriented and are related to the development strategies of a country. Therefore, the state must concentrate limited social resources through state-owned enterprises to facilitate industrialization and promote economic development. Consequently, the state-owned enterprises often played an important role in the economic development history. For example, many state-owned "model factories" were built in Prussia in the 18th century and in Japan after Meiji Restoration.[6] The nationalization in Europe after the World War II was largely related to government investment to promote post-war reconstruction and economic restoration. In developing countries such as South Korea, Brazil, Mexico and India, state-owned enterprises were also closely related to the government driving economic development through investment. With the emerging industrialized economies in East Asia as an instance, the South Korea nationalized banks in the late 1950s, which helped the government gain initiative in financing and investment in long run and thus enabled the government to support certain industries and enterprises by selective investment policies.[7] In Taiwan Province of China, the state-owned enterprises (also known as public enterprises in Taiwan) played an even more important role in the process of industrialization. From 1980 to 1983, public enterprises occupied 35% of the total industrial assets, and in 1980, among the ten biggest enterprises, seven were public enterprises. Public enterprises of Taiwan were concentrated in oil refining, petrochemical, iron and steel, ship making, machinery and chemical fertilizer industry as well as sectors of infrastructure such as power, gas, water and railway. These departments were capital intensive and linked to the factor market, which had a very close relation with the subsequent industrialization. Public enterprises also dominated the banking industry.[8] Moreover, due to relatively weaker supervision capability of the government in developing countries, in the industry of public commodities and natural monopoly, "compared to the system providing subsidies and control over private enterprises, state-owned enterprises are often more practical".[9] In addition, under the background of economic globalization, the relatively weaker national economy in developing countries can hardly compete with multinational firms of developed countries and are often merged by multinational firms. If the key sectors for the national economy or the industries related to national economic safety were controlled by foreign multinational firms, they would directly threaten the economic safety and independence of the country. Therefore, to protect the economic safety particularly the industrial safety, many developing countries establish state-owned enterprises in the mainstay industries of the national economy, strategic industries and key industries related to national economic safety, as an important institutional arrangement to defend against merger by multinational firms and realize economic independence. According to the report of the WB (1995), in 1978, the proportion of state-owned enterprises reached 8% in the eight industrialized countries and reached 23% in developing countries,[10] which demonstrates the more important role of the state-owned economy in developing countries from the statistical perspective.

Therefore, "market failure" shall not be considered as the basis for existence of the state-owned economy, and the role and scope of the state-owned economy shall not exceed the specific development stage of the country and practical issues encountered. The theories and policy suggestions acquired purely from the static market economic model are often useless. American economist Jeffrey Sachs, the designer of the "shock treatment" in the Soviet Union and Eastern Europe, who once vigorously advocated privatization, also reflected on his own and believed that the theories of privatization argued more on how state-owned enterprises declined in the process of privatization but did not pay enough attention to the role of the state-owned economy in economic growth in the earlier stage (J.D. Sachs, 1996). The Nobel Prize winner Joseph Stiglitz once pointed out that competition was far more important than privatization during economic transition and considered the idea that efficiency could be improved just by clarifying the ownership and applying privatization was a dangerous myth.[11]

However, though the state-owned economy occupies a larger proportion in the economy of developing countries, it does not mean that the state-owned economy would shrink along with economic development. The mutual alteration between privatization and nationalization trend in the economic history enlightens us that economic development of all countries may periodically rely on the state-owned economy. M. V. Posner, the famous American economist, divided the process of nationalization in the latter half of the 20th century into three stages. According to him, the first stage was "the first decade after the World War II – or to around 1960, when the state-owned economy was well applied"; the second stage was the 1960s, when the state-owned economy was not well applied, and the third stage was the 1970s, when reform of the state-owned economy was initiated. He believes that though privatization is still developing now, it was impossible to be restored to the level of privatization of the Western Europe before the World War II.[12] In view of multiple functions of the state-owned economy, in case of any change to the conditions of economic development, the role and scope of the state-owned economy would be adjusted correspondingly. The so-called nationalization policies applied by some countries in the economic crisis exactly illustrate this point.

Through the earlier discussions, we can see that the "market failure" does not constitute the basis for existence of the state-owned economy. From the point of view of "market failure", it only summarizes the function of the state-owned economy as a complement to the market mechanism, but fails to recognize its leading role and macro-significance in the national economy or explain the role and function of the state-owned economy in the socialist market economy. Then, what is the basis for existence of state-owned economy? The answer is the basic economic system at the historical stage of economic development in China.

VI.   Summary: correctly understand the basis for existence of the state-owned economy in the socialist market economy

To correctly understand the basis for existence of the state-owned economy, it is necessary to start from practices in China instead of mechanically copying theories and experiences of other countries. The state-owned economy is the leading power of the national economy, which is the fundamental positioning of the state-owned economy in the socialist market economy as well as the basic starting point to correct understand the basis for existence of the state-owned economy in the socialist market economy. To be specific, the three basic ideas shall be known as follows:

(1) From the perspective of the production relation, the leading role of the state-owned economy is manifested by the dominating position of the state-owned economy in the multiple-ownership structure, which guarantees all forms of ownership economies develop on the socialist road.

In the current stage, the public ownership of means of production consists of two major forms, ownership by the whole people and the ownership by the collective, with the former presenting in the form of state ownership. The socialist public ownership is based on the socialized large-scale production, while the highly socialized production requires all workers of the whole society uniting together to conduct uniform planned control over the means of production belonging to them according to common interests. In order to prevent the social union and occupation from becoming a mere formality, from being broken down by conflicts of partial interests and from becoming a theoretical hypothesis, an objective, humanized and tangible organization is needed to represent common interests of the society. Upon existence of the state, the state is the official representative of the whole society, and the public ownership can only be represented by the state. Therefore, in the real socialist society, it is necessary for the public ownership to present as the state ownership. Once the public ownership and the social organization of state exist, the state ownership is inevitable. Marx and Engels had once made clear explanation on this point. In the *Communist Manifesto*, they stated,

> The proletariat will make use of their political domination, capture all capitals of bourgeois step by step, concentrate all tools of production in the state organization, i.e. the proletariat that become the ruling class, and try to increase the total productivity as soon as possible.[13]

In the *Anti-Duhring*, Engels also clearly pointed out that "the proletariat will acquire the political power of the state and first turn the means of production to the state property".[14]

In the world today, no matter in the capitalist countries or socialist countries, the ownership structures are all in diverse forms, consisting of both private ownership and state ownership, and there is no pure form of single ownership. Regarding the difference, in capitalist countries, the private ownership of means of production occupies the dominating role among diverse forms of ownership, while the state-owned economy only makes a complement to the private capitals, mainly produces products that private capitals are not willing or capable to produce and provides general conditions for capital increment – the existence and proportion of which do not matter. The capitalist economic laws play the dominating role in the economic life, such as the law of capital accumulation, law of residual value and law of polarization. At the same time, in socialist countries, the public ownership of means of production takes up the dominant role, and the socialist economic characteristics or laws established based on the state-owned economy constitute the major power to support the development and changes of production relations in China, such as planned development, common prosperity, distribution on the basis of labor and meeting the growing material and cultural needs of people.

(2) From the perspective of productivity, the leading role of the state-owned economy is manifested by its control power in the national economy to

guarantee constant, coordinated and healthy development of the national economy.

The ownership structure of a state is determined by the essence of the productivity. In the current stage of China, the leading role of the state-owned economy not only reflects the essence of the socialist system but also reflects the historical requirements for the development of productivity. To be specific,

(1) During the process of industrialization and modernization, economic development has huge demands on infrastructure of energy, traffic and communication, etc. However, due to the large scale and long cycle of the investment on infrastructure, private capitals are often not willing or capable to make investment, so the construction shall be initiated by the state for the sake of long-term and overall interests and to guarantee conditions for social reproduction.
(2) To realize the overall coordinated sustainable development of the national economy, it requires the state conducting planned control over the development direction, speed, structure and major proportion of the national economy. The planned macro-control of the state can hardly be completed by private enterprises that aim to earn maximum private interests and must be completed based on the state-owned economy in a large scale.
(3) The development goal of the socialist economy is to meet the growing material and cultural needs of people. The much part of them such as the basic living demands of people or livelihood demands, as well as public social demands on science, education, culture, arts, hygiene, public undertakings and social welfare facilities showing the features of public welfare shall be guaranteed by the state-owned economy.
(4) Along with deepening economic globalization and increasingly fierce international competition, vigorous development of the state-owned economy accelerates the concentration and accumulation of domestic capitals, strengthens development and exploitation of strategic resources, helps rapid development of a batch of large multinational enterprises of international competitiveness, implements the national strategy of independent innovation, establishes the innovation-oriented country and improves the competitiveness of the state.
(5) To build a powerful socialist modernized country, it is necessary to build the powerful modernized national defense industrial system, which cannot be realized without the state-owned economy. Vigorous development of the state-owned economy is also favorable to maintaining the state sovereignty and economic security, guaranteeing the state control over key industries and areas and preventing and relieving attack of international risks.

In conclusion, the leading role of the state-owned economy plays as the important guarantee for the socialist essence of the economy in China and the constant, coordinated and healthy development of the national economy.

(3) The leading role of the state-owned economy also reflects the institutional requirement on the combination of socialism and the market economy. The role of the state-owned economy is exposed to constant changes along with the development of the productivity and production relations. In the highly concentrated planned economic system, the role and function of the state-owned economy are established through the administrative order from top to bottom. In the socialist market economy, the leading role of the state-owned economy is based on the market economic system, which reflects the requirements of the socialist system and meanwhile complies with laws of the market economy and combines the advantages of the socialist system and the market. On this issue, the follows need to be emphasized:

  (1) The state-owned economy and other ownership economies mutually promote each other and develop jointly instead of being contradicted. By adhering to the public ownership as the mainstay and giving full play to the leading role of the state-owned economy in the national economy, it is favorable to giving full play to the superiority of the socialist system, guaranteeing the socialist essence of the market economy and realizing the planned development of the state-owned economy and common social interests. Co-development of economies of different ownerships is favorable to forming the relation of equal competition among different forms of ownership, giving full play to the fundamental adjusting role of the market mechanism, mobilizing the enthusiasm and initiative of economic subjects and guaranteeing vigor of the market economy.

  (2) The leading role of the state-owned economy is mainly manifested by its control power. It is necessary to strategically adjust the layout of the state-owned economy, do what ought to do and do not do what should not do. The state-owned economy must occupy the dominating position in important industries and key areas related to the lifeline of the national economy. In other areas, it is applicable to focus on important parts through assets re-organization and structural adjustment and improve the overall quality of state-owned assets. The state-owned economy shall maintain the necessary quantity while pursue optimum layout and quality improvement. In different stages of economic development, the proportion of the state-owned economy could vary in different industries and regions, when the layout shall be correspondingly adjusted.

  (3) The leading role of the state-owned economy makes the key link for the combination of socialism and the economy. To give better play to the leading role of the state-owned economy, on the one hand, it is necessary to deepen the reform of state-owned economies, establish the state-owned economic system adapting to the market requirements and promote vigor of the state-owned economy, and, on the other hand, it is necessary to fully present the institutional advantages of the state-owned economy, give full play to the important role of the state-owned

economy in fulfilling the macro-control, safeguarding the state security, realizing equality and justice and maintaining social harmony and over-come the inherent restrictions of the market economy such as blindness, spontaneity and hysteresis and profound defects such as the economic crisis, polarization between the poor and the poor, money first and ecological damage.

(4) The leading role of the state-owned economy shall be realized by both enterprises wholly owned by the state and the state holding and joint stock enterprises in the shareholding system. Therefore, it is necessary to make the shareholding system the major form of public ownership, base on the modern ownership system, develop the mixed-ownership economy, form the pattern of equal competition and mutual promotion of diverse forms of ownership and build the modern ownership system of clear ownership and responsibilities, strict protection and smooth operation.

In conclusion, the leading role of the state-owned economy in the socialist market economy is determined by the mainstay position of the public ownership and reflects the basic system, historical stage and economic system of China. Distinguished from the capitalist economy where the state-owned economy mainly exists in the areas that private enterprises are not willing or capable to run businesses in, or is only applied as a tool of macro-control in the socialist market economy, the state-owned economy aims to promote stable, coordinated and planned development of the national economy, consolidate and improve the socialist system and realize fundamental interests of the broad masses of the people. The public ownership economy including the state-owned economy constitutes the economic foundation of the socialist system in China. If denying the mainstay position of the public ownership and the leading role of the state-owned economy, it would necessarily intensify the contradiction between labors and capitals and the polarization of wealth distribution, hasten the generation of private capitals and particularly big capitals, lead to emergence of financial oligarchy, damage social stability, result in social chaos, shake the foundation of the socialist undertakings with Chinese characteristics and, finally, impede the healthy development of the productivity. Therefore, any ambiguous idea on this issue is intolerable.

Notes

1 Zhang Xiazhun, *Hypocrisy of Rich Countries – Myth of Free Trade and Inside Story of Capitalism*, Social Science Academic Press, Edition 2009, Page 96.
2 [Australia] Hugh Stretton and Lionel Orchard, *Public Goods, Public Enterprises and Public Choices*, translated by Fei Zhaohui et al., Economic Science Press, Edition 2000, Page 149.
3 Jiang Zemin, *On Socialism With Chinese Characteristics*, CPC Archives Publishing House, Edition 2002, Page 67–69.
4 [UK] C.R. Attlee, *Will and Road Leading to Socialism*, translated by Zheng Su, The Commercial Press, Edition 1961, Page 134.

 5 [UK] Hugh Gaitskell, *Socialism and Nationalization*, translated by Li Naixi, The Commercial Press, Edition 1962, Page 25.
 6 Zhang Xiazhun, *Hypocrisy of Rich Countries – Myth of Free Trade and Inside Story of Capitalism*, Social Science Academic Press, Edition 2009, Page 103.
 7 Alice H. Amsden, *Asia's Next Giant*. Oxford University Press, 1989, Page 73–75.
 8 [US] Robert Wade, *Driving the Market*, translated by Lv Xingjian et al., Beijing: Enterprise Management Publishing House, Edition 1994, Page 191–197.
 9 Zhang Xiazhun, *Hypocrisy of Rich Countries – Myth of Free Trade and Inside Story of Capitalism*, Social Science Academic Press, Edition 2009, Page 105.
10 The World Bank, *Researches on Government-Operated Enterprises – Economics and Politics on Reform of State-owned Enterprises*, China Financial and Economic Publishing House, Edition 1997, Page 7.
11 Joseph E. Stigliz, *Whither Socialism*, The MIT Press, 1994, Page 160.
12 [UK] John Eatwell, Murray Milgate, and Peter Newman, *The New PalGrave Dictionary Of Economics*, Vol. 3, translated by Chen Daisun et al., Economic Science Press, Edition 1992, Page 640.
13 *Selected Works of Marx and Engels*, Vol. 1, People's Publishing House, Edition 1995, Page 286.
14 *Selected Works of Marx and Engels*, Vol. 3, People's Publishing House, Edition 1995, Page 630.

6 The relationship between government and market in the socialist market economy

I. Introduction

The relationship between government and market is the core issue of the economic system. The traditional planned economic system is characterized by the unclear division of the government and enterprises, where the government controls the right to make decisions on both macro-economy and micro-economy. The transition from the planned economy to the socialist market economy requires the separation of the government and enterprises, the division between the macro-control by the government and micro-activities by enterprises and the change of the major task of the government from the direct control over enterprises to the planned control over the macro-economy. The transition has experienced the following four major development stages in general:

(1) The 12th National Congress of the CPC emphasized "the leading role of the planned economy and the supplementary role of market regulation" and stressed that the planned control played the fundamental and major role and the market control played the subordinate and secondary role.
(2) The 13th National Congress of the CPC proposed to establish the planned commodity economy and emphasized that the new operating mechanism was "the government controlling the market and the market guiding enterprises".
(3) The report from the 14th National Congress of the CPC put forward the reform goal as establishment of the socialist market economic system and emphasized, "The socialist market economic system as our goal is to give play to the fundamental role of the market in the allocation of resources under the macro-control by the socialist government".
(4) The 3rd Plenary Session of the 18th Central Committee of the CPC put forward the theory of "giving play to the decisive role of the market in the allocation of resources and giving better play to the role of the government" and emphasized that the "decisive role" inherited and developed the "fundamental role".

As indicated by the aforementioned process of understanding, our understanding about the relationship between government and market in the socialist market economy is constantly deepening and improving. Despite all this, there are still arguments and divergences in the academic circle and actual work on how to accurately master the relationship between government and market theoretically and practically. For example, some scholars believe that the decisive role of the market in allocation of resources means that the government shall completely quit from allocation of resources, have its economic function restricted to providing public services to the market economy and play the complementary role in economic development. Some other scholars suggest not unilaterally understand and exaggerate the decisive role of the market.

Some scholars believe that it is necessary to clarify the fundamental difference between the decisive role of the government in the socialist market economy and the market determinism of the western neoliberalism. The first is the co-existence of the macro-control by the government and the micro-regulation. Second, the market is restricted to short-term allocation of general allocations and does not play a part in the allocation of special resources such as non-underground resources and long-term allocation of general resources. Third, the allocation of non-material resources such as culture and education requires the introduction of the market mechanism applicable to this area and shall not be decided by the market. The fourth is the public ownership as the mainstay and state-owned economy as the guide, which is reflected by the market economic system and market activities. Fifth, the market and government, respectively, play their adjusting role in the distribution of wealth and income, while the market plays a bigger part in initial distribution of the national income and the government plays a bigger part in re-distribution.[1]

Moreover, some scholars propose that the allocation of resources is divided into different levels, including the macro- and micro-level, and is categorized in different fields. In terms of the micro-level of allocation of resources – i.e., the allocation of multiple types of resources among various market entities – the law of the market value could promote efficiency through changes of the supply and demand and the competition mechanism and play a very important role, or, a "decisive" role. However, in the macro-level of allocation of resources such as the comprehensive balance of the total supply and demand, proportional structure of sectors and areas, protection of natural resources and environment and equality in social distribution, as well as allocation of resources related to national and social security and people's welfare (housing, education and medical care), etc., it shall not rely on the market for adjustment, not to mention its "decisive role". The market mechanism is subject to many defects and weaknesses in the macro-area, where the state intervention, government management and planned control are required to correct, restrict and complement the market behaviors, thus to apply the "visible hand" to make up the defects of the "invisible hand".[2]

Some other scholars also put forward that the market economy has two models, the capitalist market economy and the socialist market economy. The market economy is not born as capitalist or socialist. If the allocation of resources in the micro and macro-economic areas in China are both completely decided by the market and no restriction is imposed on the development of the market economy, where will it finally lead to? It is for sure that it will not lead to consolidation and development of the socialist public ownership economy, the perfection and development of the basic economic system, the elimination of the polarization between the poor and the rich or the equality in income distribution, people-oriented scientific development or realization of the common prosperity. In summary, it will not lead to consolidation and development of socialism.[3]

Therefore, it is a critical issue in current economic theories and practices that how to deal with the relationship between government and market during the process of deepening reform of the economic system, which needs us to conduct in-depth research based on Chinese practices with Marxist theories as the guide, thus to attain theoretical breakthroughs and promote the development of practices.

II. Three dimensions for understanding and dealing with the relationship between government and market

Is there a universal optimum model for dealing with the relationship between government and market? The answer is no. This is because the government and the market are both in a social and historical range, which are subject to a process of dynamic changes along with development of the social productivity, relations of production and superstructure. For example, the socialist country is different from the capitalist country, the developing country is different from the developed country and the big country is different from the small country. Even in the capitalist markets with the same degree of development shows different models in different regions, including the free market economy in America, the corporate monopoly market economy in Japan, the social market economy in Germany and the welfare market economy in Sweden.

To correctly understand the relationship between government and market in the socialist market economy, it is necessary to proceed from the reality of China and master three major dimensions:

The first is the general laws of the market economy, with the law of value as the core, which adjusts production and allocates resources through supply, competition and price fluctuation in the market mechanism. However, even in developed market economies, the government also plays an indispensable role. On the one hand, the market mechanism only plays its part under certain conditions, including the legal system, competition rules, macro-environment and social security, etc., which are formed and improved based on the role of the government. On the other hand, the market economy is exposed to weaknesses such as partial failure as well as blindness, spontaneity and hysteresis, and the government plays a significant role in complementing the market failure and overcoming market defects.

The second is the national conditions and development stage. The market in reality is not an abstract concept, but a specific existence in certain time and space subject to influence of technical, economic, legal, political, historical and cultural factors. Being a developing big power, China has vast land and a large population and is characterized by thick and unique cultural traditions, backward development of productivity, imbalance in regional development, long-term existence of the dual structure and the long historical process of transition from the planned economy to the market economy. The special social and historical conditions necessarily bring about extremely big influence on the relationship between government and market.

The third is the basic system in China. The basic economic system refers to the essence and structure of the ownership of means of production, which is the core ad foundation of a social and economic system as well as the major factor that decides the relationship between government and market. China adopts the socialist market economy – i.e., the market economy combining the basic socialist system. The socialist market economy shall comply with general laws of the market economy and meanwhile reflect the requirements of the basic socialist system. In this way, the government and the market are given new characteristics. Compared to the government in the capitalist country, the government in the socialist country has different essence, function and operating model. Compared to the market in the capitalist country, the market in the socialist country has a different status, role and operating laws.

In conclusion, the market economy in China is the socialist market economy in a big power under development and transition, which is the basic fact that we must understand so as to correctly understand the relationship between government and market in China.

III. The government and the market are supplementary to each other instead of being opposite to each other

When understanding and dealing with the relationship between government and market, people often stress more on the opposition and contradiction between the two, believing that the market is effective and the government is ineffective, so consider it necessary to weaken or even cancel the role of government to give play to the role of the market mechanism and advocate the large market, small government and privatization. This idea only sees the opposite side between government and market but fails to recognize the supplementary effect between government and market.

The relationship between government and market is essentially the relation between the society and individuals and between public interests and private interests. Being the sum of the commodity exchange relations, the market reflects the economic relation among independent commodity producers. As stated by Karl Marx, "things are used as commodities because they are products of private labors which are independent from each other", and "both parties of the exchange must admit that the counterparty is the private owner".[4] However, the government or the state is the social center and the representative of social interests. In the class society, the government is first the center of the class rule and the representative of the class interests. Therefore, at first glance, the government and market are opposite to each other and show clear boundary. It is necessary to respect the rights and benefits of private producers and consumers thus to respect laws of the market, otherwise it will break the laws of market and inhibit the market vitality. In this way, liberals put forward that the society coming very naturally is the best society, and it will naturally reach the sum of private interests – i.e., the common interests when everyone is pursuing for their own private interests – so it will be better if the government exerts less control and the government intervention in economy is unnecessary and harmful.

However, this is only a superficial understanding, and the fact speaks in the other way around. In the competition of the market economy, "everyone is hindering others from realizing their interests. The war of everyone opposing everyone only results in general negation instead of general recognition".[5] It means that the pursuit of private interests would not necessarily acquire social interests, but would damage social interests on the contrary. The government should play the active role instead of exerting less control. The conclusion can be drawn if we understand the essence of the market economy.

The market economy emerges and develops based on labor division and private ownership, which, on the one hand, leads to separation of different producers, and, on the other hand, results in mutual dependence among them. In this way, the basic conflict of the market economy emerges – i.e., the conflict between private labor and social labor. It provides the internal driving force for the development of the market economy and, meanwhile, gives rise to various factors that deny the market economy; individual enterprises are organizational, while the whole social production is anarchic, leading to disjoint of production and consumption and disproportion among different departments; the production shows the tendency of unlimited expansion and the market demand is relatively restricted due to contradiction between labor and capital, leading to periodic outbreak of economic crisis of overproduction; the free competition applies the law of jungle, necessarily brings about survival of the fittest and the polarization, intensifies social conflicts and confrontation and breaks social harmony and stability; universal development of the commodity relation incorporates people's basic demands and basic values such as life and health, culture and education, nature and environment, safety and freedom in the scope of commercialization makes them the appurtenance to capitals and factors to production and threatens people's common interests; free competition necessarily leads to centralization and monopoly of production, while it would hinder or even eliminate competition and break up the foundation for market economy when it reaches certain degree. These profound defects contained in the market economy cannot be overcome by themselves but are only subject to government and social regulation. We shall also see that the government plays a limited role and could not solve every difficulty due to its own weaknesses. However, there is no doubt that the government is the most important and indispensable approach to overcome defects of the market economy.

In this way, the government and market seem contradicted to each other from the perspective of micro individuals, and it would be better if the government exerts less control. However, from the macro-social perspective, it can be seen that the government and the market are not contradicted but are complementary to each other. The market economy in developing countries is backward and immature, manifested by weak market role such as the incomplete market system, chaos of the market order and distorted price signal, as well as weak role of the government such as government incompetence, law relaxation and corruption, where the market economy necessarily lacks efficiency. In general, the government is playing a part far exceeding the "night watch" in the modern market economy. The strength of a government has become a decisive factor determining the international status and international competition of the government.

IV. Clarification on several popular ideas about the role of government

In terms of the relationship between government and market, some currently popular ideas are incorrect and need to be clarified.

Some people believe that the government regulation and market regulation show clear boundary and are subject to the game relationship and the reform of the economic system is giving the power of government to the market to realize the complete market-oriented allocation of resources and social operation. The earlier idea only describes the market economy in a highly abstract and simple way but fails to comprehensively and accurately reflect the truth of the market economy. The market economy in reality is much more complicated. In addition to government and market, enterprises, particularly the large enterprises, also make the important organizations to allocate resources. Moreover, the political organization, social organization, legal system and conventional morality also show important impact on allocation of resources. Meanwhile, many important intermediary organizations exist between the government and the market. For example, state-owned enterprises not only constitute market entities but also bear important responsibilities to exert government regulation, and the local government plays the part of both the governmental organization and the entrepreneur. Particular emphasis is given to the Party leadership, which is the most essential feature of the socialism with Chinese characteristics. The core role of the Party in overall planning and coordination of various aspects constitutes a significant characteristic of the socialist market economic system in China as well as the important guarantee for the development of the socialist market economic development. Therefore, it is a complicated systematic project to improve the market economic system, which demands cooperation of various aspects including the government, market, laws, morality and the political system reform.

Some people believe that the optimum model for the market economy is the "big market and small government". This idea puts the government and the market in contradicted positions against each other, believes that the market is effective and the government is ineffective and so considers it necessary to weaken or even cancel the role of government. However, what decides that it is a good or a bad government is not about whether it is big or small, but is about whether it is powerful or weak. The government that fully fulfills its social function and represents social interests is the powerful government, while the government that fails to fulfill its social function and represent social interests is the weak government. In fact, the government is bearing increasingly more economic functions and growing larger during development from early capitalism to modern capitalism. Far beyond the scope of "night watch", the government has widely involved in various fields of the economy and society, and the liberal ideal of "big market and small government" has already become historical relic.

Some people believe that the government is the referee instead of the player in the market economy and so shall bear more functions in addition to formulating the market rules and maintaining the market order. This idea appears right but is in fact wrong and confusing. Indeed, from the perspective of the market transaction and market competition, the government is no doubt the referee instead of the player. However, is there no other economic issue in a society other than transaction and competition? If considering it from the perspective such as economic development, international competition, guarantee of people's living standards and improvement of the socialist system, it can be seen that the government is not only the referee but also the important organizer, starter and participant, which acts as the leading power.

Some people believe that the government mainly plays the part to make up the market failure – i.e., exerting administrative regulation or control over the market in case of failure of the market mechanism, such as monopoly, externality, public commodities and information asymmetry. This is only the idea of microeconomics. Practically, the major defects of the market economy exist in the macro-level instead of the micro-level. From the macro-perspective, according to the Marxist economics, the basic capitalist conflict is the conflict between production socialization and private capitalist ownership of means of production, which is specifically manifested by the contradiction of the capital and labor, polarization between the poor and the rich, unemployment and economic crisis and unorganized economic operation. Keynesianism and the government intervention theory in contemporary capitalist countries also admit this point.

Some people believe that the government mainly plays its role in macro-control – i.e., formulating and implementing policies on and maintaining stability of macro-economy. This proposal is also incomplete. Macro-control constitutes only one part of the economic function of the government, which actually consists of some other important economic functions such as micro-regulation, market supervision and public services. Meanwhile, the government in the socialist economy also features some special economic functions, such as planned coordination, overall planning and management of state-owned assets and the economic functions related to the special national conditions and the development stage of China, such as economic development, structural adjustment and institutional innovation, which are not reflected by the concept of macro-control.

Some people believe that the role of government in the market economy is providing services and it is the main direction for transformation of the governmental system to the "service-oriented government". However, the key issue lies in the object of the service. It is correct if the object is the masses and the goal is to build the government serving the people. However, if the service object is the enterprise (practically capitals) according to the popular idea now, it would become a very difficult issue. The "service-oriented government" we are stressing now is not the complete conclusion of the role or function of the government in the socialist market economy, but intends to strengthen the service awareness and level of the government, reduce and regulate on administrative approval and weaken the government intervention in the micro-economic operation.

The fundamental error of the aforementioned popular ideas is that they mechanically copy the stale rules of western new and old liberalism; deny the positive role of the government; put the government and market in totally contradicted positions; break away from basic national conditions, institution and development stage of China; violate against objective laws of economic development; and fail to comply with fundamental interests of the broad masses of the people.

V.   Model of state intervention beyond Keynesianism

The laissez-faire policy can no longer adapt to economic development after the World War II, when the state interventionism of Keynesianism emerged as the times required and became the popular economic system of developed capitalist countries. Basic features of Keynesian state interventionism system consist of the following: (1) enterprises are independent micro-economic entities, while the major function of the government is to conduct indirect macro-control over economic operation; (2) the balance between the total supply and total demand is the basic goal of indirect control; (3) the fiscal and monetary policies play as the basic measure for indirect control. In this mode, resources are allocated completely based on the market economy, while the government only plays a role in maintaining the exterior conditions for market operation and creating a normal environment for the role of the market mechanism. This is the mode of market economy of indirect macro-coordination in the total volume.[6] This model of state intervention in western countries is praised highly by many people and is considered as the standard for the advanced market economy. Quite a lot of scholars have proposed the basic principles for the government's role in the market economy in China based on this model – i.e., the government only controls the value but not material objects, the total amount but not the structure, the macro-economy but not the micro-level and the demand but not the supply. It shall be acknowledged that the model of state intervention in developed capitalist countries provides a certain standard to the construction of the market economic system in China and is of great significance as the reference. However, this model incorporates some fundamental defects and does not meet practical conditions of China and shall not be mechanically copied.

First, the model lacks the long-term plan for economic development. The long-term policies of a state shall be made based on the long-term interests of economic development, which directly determine the development direction, speed and overall structure of the national economy and are not subject to regulation by the short-term fluctuation of market prices. The government mainly realizes long-term decisions through direct regulation measures such as industrial policies and government investment. In comparison, in the model of the market economy under regulation, the major task of the government control is to overcome market fluctuation and maintain stability and balance of macro-economy and does not consider about long-term development, presenting obvious defects for developing countries like China.

Second, this model lacks the measures to realize the long-term goal of economic development. In general, the economic development structure formulated based on long-term interests of economic development by the state is always inconsistent with the economic structure spontaneously generated in the market. The inconsistency exactly makes the planned control necessary. However, realization of the goal of the planned control cannot completely rely on direct management on total demand, because it is only a short-term policy on total volume but is incapable of conducting long-term structural adjustment. The direct control by the government is needed more to realize the long-term goal of economic development.

Third, this model lacks the measures to cope with market failure in underdeveloped market economy. In the developed market economy, market failure is mainly a kind of partial dysfunction, but in the underdeveloped market economy like China, due to incomplete market development and distorted market signal, the market failure goes much wider and deeper than that in countries of developed market economy. Under these circumstances, the controlling role of the market mechanism in resources allocation is subject to greater restrictions, and the control and intervention by the government in the economic life is wider and deeper than that in countries of developed market economy.

Fourth, during the transition from the planned economy to the market economy, China is encountered with various conflicts and contradictions including population expansion, deterioration of ecological environment, backward infrastructure, rising unemployment rate, expanding income gap, fierce international competition and contradiction between new and old ideas. Under the special historical conditions, without a powerful government that safeguards national independence, social stability, strict legislation system and economic prosperity, the economy and society would fall into serious chaos and disorder, and reform and development would be hindered.

Fifth, as a developing country, China cannot fulfill the catch-up task as a latecomer country in industrialization through spontaneous evolution. It requires the leading role of the government, facilitating concentration and accumulation of domestic capitals, promoting rapid expansion of key sectors and key enterprises, accelerating re-organization of the industrial structure and hi-tech development, improving the international competitiveness of the national economy and trying to narrow the gap with developed countries. The backward Chinese economy holds an unfavorable position in international competition. Under these conditions, if without a powerful government that represents and safeguards the overall interests of the state, it is difficult to avoid the disastrous consequence of coherent imitativeness, separation and dependence in modernization of developing countries.

Sixth, the socialist market economy in China adheres to the public ownership as the mainstay. Despite the great change to the ownership structure during economic transition and the great development of the proportion of non-public ownership and non-state-owned economy, the basic socialist economic system adhering to the mainstay position of public ownership will not be exposed to fundamental changes. In this kind of economic system, the government not only bears the responsibility to control the macro-economy but also involves in the process of economic operation as the owner of means of production, which is the fundamental difference between the socialist market economic system in China and the western market economic system under state intervention.

Therefore, the indirect control model of Keynesianism cannot solve economic issues in China. The model of the market economy that complies with the national conditions in China must link general rules of the market economy to practical conditions in China; combine the planned control and the market control; direct control and indirect control; supply management and demand management, short-term goal and long-term goal and total balance and structure optimization; and give full play to both the regulating role of the market mechanism and the leading role of the government in economic and social development.

VI. Major role of the government in the socialist market economy

Then, what role should the state play in the socialist market economy exactly? The follows shall be included:

(1) Overall planned arrangement. As the market mechanism presents inherent defects of spontaneity, blindness and hysteresis, the state shall conduct planned control and overall arrangement for the national economic and social development based on overall and long-term interests thus to reduce the negative influence of these defects of the market mechanism on economic development. The overall planned arrangement is the most fundamental and the highest economic function of the state, which aims to conduct planned control over the goal, structure, speed and result of national economic and social development from the macro-level. In addition, it is designed to make overall plan on urban and rural development, regional development, economic and social development, harmonious development of man and nature, domestic development and opening to the outside, personal interests and collective interests, partial interests and overall interests, current interests and long-term interests, and promote economic development in a rapid and favorable way.

(2) Public service. The public service refers to the basic non-profitable products and services provided for all residents of the society, including national defense, security, public medical care, public education, social security, environmental protection and infrastructure construction, etc. Though these basic products and services constitute the important guarantee for economic and social development, they cannot be effectively satisfied by the market mechanism due to their special non-profitable attribute and must be rendered by the government. The new driving force can only be provided for economic growth by accelerating construction of the public services-oriented

government, creating favorable environment of laws and policies and orderly and competitive order for economic development, strengthening public management, guaranteeing full supply of public products and public services and realizing social equality and justice.

(3) Macro-control. The imbalance of macro-economy is an inherent defect of the market economy. Under the market economy, the balance between production and demands is spontaneously controlled through the price mechanism, which, however, cannot guarantee the balance between total production and total demand of the whole society and may lead to mass unemployment of workers and vicious inflation under certain conditions. The market failure in the macro-level requires the government controlling the aggregate relation and promoting the balance of macro-economy, such as promoting the aggregate balance of the national economy and price stabilization by controlling the total supply and total demand through fiscal and monetary policies, improving employment through macro-control over the labor market and employment policies, realizing balance on international income and expenditure through macro-control over international income and expenditure and facilitating stable and healthy development of the national economy through economic reverse regulation to eliminate the fluctuation in economic operation.

(4) Micro-control. The failure of the market mechanism is another important defect of the market economy, mainly manifested by the externality, monopoly, information asymmetry and public products, etc. In case of market failure, the role of the market mechanism in allocation of resources would be restricted. In this case, the government control is also required, such as controlling the external diseconomy and making use of external economic effects through government intervention, creating the fair and competitive environment for the market and the market order and promoting generation of the effective market structure by preparing rules for market entry, market transaction and market exit as well as unfair competition and anti-monopoly measures, and relieving the danger on economic efficiency brought about by system asymmetry by improving transparency and supply of the transaction information. Since the government intervention often directly involves in the market through non-market measure in the micro-level, it replaces or restricts the role of the market and is therefore called the micro-control.

(5) Supervision and management of state-owned assets. In the socialist market economy, the state-owned economy plays the leading role in the development of the national economy and occupies relatively greater proportion in some key areas and important industries. Under these circumstances, as the owner of the state-owned economy, the government shall bear the responsibility to represent all people to conduct effective supervision and management of state-owned assets, guarantee maintenance and appreciation of the value of state-owned assets, manage assets and stocks of state-owned economy through state-owned assets management organizations and agencies, appoint or nominate the responsible person for companies controlled by the state,

involve in decision-making of major strategies for operation of state-owned assets and supervise operation of state-owned enterprises. This is an important duty of the government in the socialist market economy.

(6) Institutional innovation. In a socialist country under development and transformation, it is an important function for the socialist state to lead and organize reform and promote institutional innovation. Distinguished from the development history of capitalism in the early stage, the socialist system is built and develops in an independent endogenous way, namely through a planned and organized way under the leadership of the Party and the government. Moreover, the Party and government has also led and initiated the reform and improvement of the socialist system such as the transition from the planned economy to the socialist market economy since Reform and Opening Up. Therefore, the state is the leading power for not only the economic development but also reform and development of the market economy and institutional innovation. The economic reform in China is also a kind of government-guided institutional change.

(7) Guarantee of people's livelihood. As pointed out by the report from the CPC 17th National Congress,

> Based on economic development, attach more importance to social construction, put great efforts to guarantee and improve people's livelihood, promote reform of the social system, expand public services, perfect social management, enhance social equality and justice, endeavor to guarantee education, labor remuneration, medical care, elderly care and housing of people ad promote construction of the harmonious society.

The construction of people's livelihood mainly provides public commodities, which cannot be fully controlled by the market mechanism since it aims to satisfy people's basic demands instead of pursuing maximum profits. Therefore, only the state-owned economy can bear responsibilities in the area related to construction of people's livelihood such as public medical care, public education, affordable housing, water supply, power supply, energy supply and communication service.

(8) Regulation of income distribution. The socialist system is built based on the public ownership of means of production, while the essential requirement of socialism is to realize common prosperity. However, the common prosperity cannot be realized by merely the market economy. The market economy adheres to the "the law of the jungle". Particularly in the capitalist market economy, the general law of capital accumulation presents as the polarization of the wealth occupation, where the wealth is accumulated and expanded among a few people and most people are leading a relatively poorer life. Encountered with the severe weaknesses of the market economy, the capitalist countries adhering to the doctrine of freedom first must turn to state interventionism and bear the responsibility in adjusting the income distribution and establishing the social security and welfare system. In this way, to realize

common prosperity of the society, it is necessary to strengthen re-distribution of incomes including improving the social security system, increasing public expenditure and intensifying transfer payment and facilitate improvement of the re-distribution adjusting mechanism with taxation, social security and transfer payment as the major measure. However, distinguished from capitalist countries, realization of common prosperity in the socialist economy relies on not only the re-distribution of the national income by the state but also the guarantee of the basic socialist system and socialist distribution system. Adjustment by the government on income distribution makes up an important condition for realization of common prosperity and integration of efficiency and justice.

These functions reflect both general laws of the market economy and special requirements on the socialist system. It can be seen that the relation between the government and the market in the socialist market economy has rich connotations. It plays a key role in consolidating and improving the socialist system and realizing fundamental interests of all people and constitutes an important condition for healthy development and effective operation of the socialist market economy to well fulfill these functions of the government.

VII. Competent party and government and effective market – guided by the government in the macro-way and determined by the market in the micro-way

A basic conclusion can be drawn from the earlier discussion that in the socialist market economy, the market mainly plays its decisive role in the micro-economic area and the leadership of the Party and the leading role of the government shall be emphasized from the perspective from of social development and macro-economy.

The market economy is the economic system where the allocation of resources is regulated by the market mechanism – i.e., through the role of the supply and demand, price and competition. In this sense, the decisive role of the market is the general law and essential feature of the market economy. However, the scope and conditions for the decisive role of the market vary significantly under different social systems.

In the simple commodity economy, the whole social economy and social order are subject to non-market principles such as blood relationship, rank and power, and the decisive role of the market is mainly reflected in the small commodity economy. In comparison, in the capitalist market economy, the decision role of the market is reflected by not only the commodity production and commodity exchange but also the allocation of production factors such as capitals, labors and natural resources, not only the micro-level – i.e., the adjustment of the market on economic activities of producers and consumers – but also the macro-level – i.e., the adjustment on all sectors of the whole society and various economic relations, and not only the economic area but also all aspects of the social life. The decisive role of the market is fundamentally the decisive role of capitals, so the capital dominates the whole social economy, politics and culture, etc. Special laws of the capitalist economy such as the law of residential value, capital accumulation and equalization of profit have become the general laws of the market economy. The basic conflict of capitalism and its pattern of manifestation such as class antagonism, economic crisis and polarization have become increasingly intensified along with the development of capitalism. As the main representative of the bourgeoisie, capitalist countries have to conduct direct and indirect intervention on the economy to guarantee the stability and constant development of the economy and maintain overall interests of capitals. However, the intervention in the economy by capitalist countries always faces the fundamental conflict due to restrictions imposed by the private ownership that the too weak government intervention can hardly solve the severe issues coherent in the capitalist market economy including unemployment, economic crisis and polarization, etc., and the too strong government intervention will damage the principle of the sanctity of private ownership. As proved by facts, various measures adopted by capitalist countries to solve the crises only make these crises show up again on a larger scale. The capitalist market economy based on private ownership cannot realize the real and effective government intervention. As Karl Marx pointed out at an earlier time, "The sticking point of the bourgeois society lies in no conscious regulation on production since the beginning".[7] Any conscious social supervision and adjustment during social production is regarded as an infringement upon the capitalists' property right, freedom and "originality" of self-determination.

With a great difference, the socialist market economy regards public ownership as the foundation. The control of the socialist government on the economy is derived from not only the exterior administrative intervention by the state but also the internal requirements of production relations, as the production relations of the public ownership require rational allocation of resources within the scope of the whole society based on common interests of the society and overcoming the conflict between socialization of production and capitalist private ownership of means of production. Consciousness and planning of the social development are the essential characteristics and the fundamental superiority of the socialist system.

Under the socialist market economic conditions, from the perspective of the micro-economy, both private enterprises and public enterprises pursue for maximum profits and both are subject to adjustment by the market system. It means that the market plays the decisive role in allocation of resources. However, for the whole society, the goal of production development or resources allocation is no longer to pursue maximum profits, but to satisfy material and cultural demands of people to the maximum extent and realize the all-around development of people and achieve common prosperity of the whole society. It is obviously insufficient to merely rely on the market regulation to realize the goal. The market can only realize the short-term and private demands with capability in currency payment, but social plan and the role of government are indispensable for satisfying the common and long-term interests of the masses.

Which aspects reflect the leading role of the government in the macro-level?

Which aspects reflect the leading role of the state in the socialist market economy?

The first is the leadership by the Party. The Communist Party of China is the core of leadership in the construction of the socialist undertakings with Chinese characteristics. The role of Party in overall planning and coordination and economic guidelines, principles and policies under the leadership of the Party lead the development direction of the national economy in general and guarantee the constant and healthy development of the national economy.

The second is the plan, layout and strategy for the national economy and social development. The plan, layout and strategy refer to the overall and fundamental principle that guides economic development and reflect the overall and fundamental interests of social members, which constitute the general basis for guidance on the development of the national economy.

The third is the basic socialist economic system. The basic economic system that keeps public ownership as the mainstay of the economy and allows diverse forms of ownership to develop side by side is the foundation for the socialist market economy, which determines all links of the socialist economy including production, distribution and exchange as well as the interest relations and modes of act of all economic entities.

The fourth is the leading role of the state-owned economy. By giving play to the leading role of the state-owned economy, it is favorable to assuring the control power of the government on economy and society, diverse forms of ownership developing along the socialist road and the national economy developing as planned in good proportion and provides the important guarantee for realizing fundamental interests and common prosperity of the masses.

The fifth is the all-around goal of control. The control of the socialist country on the economy aims not only to complement the market failure but also to realize economic development, aggregate balance, structure optimization, market efficiency, guarantee of people's livelihood, beautiful environment, social equality and common prosperity, etc.

The sixth is the control mode at multiple levels. The control by socialist countries on the economy is not restricted to relieving short-term issues, but perfect combines the planned control and market control, direct control and indirect control, aggregate balance and structure evolution and long-term goal and short-term goal.

In this way, from the perspective of macro-economy and overall development, it is the leadership of the Party and the role of government instead of the market which plays the decisive role in the socialist market economy. It is the outstanding feature of the relation between the government and market in the socialist market economy that combines the decisive role of the market at the micro-level and the leading role of the state at the macro-level.

VIII.   Stress on laws of the market and give better play to the government

The macro-control by the government and the fundamental role of the market system, being internally integrated, constitute the essential requirements of the socialist market economic system. It is the mainline running through the reform of the economic system as well as the breakthrough point for improving the core of the socialist market economic system and deepening reform to well deal with the relation between the government and the market. At the current stage, to improve the socialist market economic system, it is necessary to consciously abide by objective economic laws, deepen the economic system reform with the relation between the government and the market as its center, guarantee the fundamental role of the market in allocation of resources, give full play to the role of the government in macro-control and combine the effective market control and the effective government control, thus to show forth the superiority of the socialist system, further realize integrity of equality and efficiency and render constant vigor and driving force for economic development.

As the core in deepening reform, the relation between the government and the market involves all aspects of the economic system, including enterprises, prices, finance and taxation, banking, administrative management, income distribution and social security, etc., with any aspect that may affect the whole situation. Two current issues on the relationship between the government and the market shall be recognized. The first issue is the over control by the government of micro-economic activities and the insufficient role of the market system, such as too wide scope subject to the administrative approval by the government; concentrated power; inorganized arrangement for prices of some important resources; severe administrative tendency in operation and management of state-owned enterprises and units; separation of the urban and rural system; and the incomplete market of production factors. The other issue is that some things that need control are not well controlled, and the role of the government has not been well played, such as the schedule, efficiency and authority of macro-control by the government needing to be improved, environmental pollution and issue on food and medicine security, imperfect market supervision, weak control over income distribution of polarization, incomplete construction of people's livelihood and social security, unconsolidated basic economic system and severe corruption of power-money transaction. These two issues are both prominent and shall be attached equal importance to theoretically and practically.

Therefore, it shall start from two aspects to correctly deal with the relation between the government and the market: on the one hand, promote reform in relevant fields based on greater respect to laws of the market, further simplify the administration and delegate power to lower levels, improve the market system, perfect the mechanism for pricing of production factors and resources, facilitate the free flow of factors between the urban and rural area and promote the market vitality, and, on the other hand, promote reform in relevant fields based on giving better play to the role of the government; further improve the fiscal and taxation system, financial supervision system and macro-control system; deepen reform of the administrative management system; drive development of scientific and democratic decision making; strengthen mechanism construction of the macro-control goal and policies and measures; improve the schedule, efficiency and authority of macro-control; safeguard equality and justice; promote common prosperity and better combine the visible hand and the invisible hand; and further give play to the institutional advantages of the socialist market economy and enable the economy to develop in a more efficient, fair and sustainable way.

Notes

1 Cheng Enfu, "Clarify the Two Theories on Market Determinism", *Global Times*, December 10, 2013.
2 Liu Guoguang, "Two Levels of Allocation of Resources and Dual Role of the Government and Market", *Social Sciences Weekly*, January 5, 2014.
3 Wei Xinghua, "Different Essence of the Macro Allocation of Resources and the Micro Allocation of Resources", *Review on Political Economics*, 2014, 4th Issue, Page 3–14.
4 Karl Marx, *Capital*, Vol. 1, People's Publishing House, Edition 2004, Page 90.
5 Karl Marx, *Critique of Political Economics (Manuscripts of 1857–1858)*: *Selections of Marx and Engels*, Vol. 30, People's Publishing House, Edition 1995, Page 106.
6 Though the governments in western developed countries also formulate a few supply policies, structure policies and micro-regulation policies, they are still far from becoming the mainstream.
7 Karl Marx, *From Karl Marx to Ludwig Kugelmann*, July 11, 1986, Vol. 4 of *Selected Works of Marx and Engels*, People's Publishing House, Edition 2012, Page 474.

7 Reasons for the constant and rapid development of the Chinese economy

Since the Reform and Opening Up, Chinese economy has attained the constant rapid growth with an average annual rate of approximately 10% and created a miracle of development. Then, what are the major reasons contributing to this miracle? Currently, Chinese economy has ushered in the "new normal" and has the economic growth rate transit from the ultra-high speed to the medium-high speed. Will the transition change the historical trend of constant rapid development of Chinese economy? This is an important question to answer so as to scientifically summarize experiences on economic reform in China and accurately judge the development trend of Chinese economy.

I. The period of strategic opportunities for rapid development of China has not ended yet

According to general laws of economic development, the rapid growth emerges mostly during the process of industrialization, urbanization and modernization, and the room for economic growth shrinks and rapid growth ends only after completion of industrialization, urbanization and modernization. This is mainly because during industrialization and urbanization, production factors transfer from the agricultural sector of lower productivity to the industrial sector of higher productivity; the overall efficiency of resources allocation improves and the agricultural population transferring to the urban area and other industries creates huge social demands, which stimulates the development of the industry and the service sector; promotes product innovation and industrial upgrading; and drives the all-around development of social undertakings including science, technology, culture, education, sports and medical system, etc. Based on development experiences of late-advanced economies such as Japan, South Korea and China Taiwan, they have experienced the rapid economic growth for two or three decades during industrialization and urbanization, with an annual growth rate reaching or exceeding 9%.

China has attained great achievements in industrialization, urbanization and modernization in over 60 years since foundation of New China, particularly in over 30 years since the Reform and Opening Up. By now, industrialization has stepped into the stage of middle and later development but is still far from completion. Potentials in industrialization, urbanization and modernization are far from being completely released.

First, from the perspective of the degree of industrialization development in China, despite there being no universal criteria for judgment on the specific industrialization index, it is generally believed that industrialization in China is in the later phase of the middle stage – i.e., just getting across the middle stage, and is transiting from heavy industrialization to high-processing stage. In this stage, the production method of the whole society becomes more circuitous, the industrial chain significantly extends and the driving ability of the industrial sector in the upper and downstream is vigorously strengthened. In the current stage, China is leading a new industrialization road where industrialization and informatization are combined and mutually promoted, and its potential and energy of development run rings around traditional industrialization.

Second, from the perspective of urbanization degree, the urbanization rate in China was 17.9% in 1978 and rose to 56.1% by 2015, suggesting rapid development of urbanization. According to the goal in the *National New Urbanization Planning (2014–2020)*, the urbanization rate should attain around 60% by 2020 and 70% by 2030, when the urbanization would be basically realized. Therefore, urbanization still sees a great room for growth. In the current stage, the urbanization in China is the new style of urbanization of overall planning on, interaction between and integration of the rural and urban area, rational layout, land preservation and complete function, with its development potential and energy far beyond the traditional urbanization.

Third, in terms of modernization, the per-capita GDP of China in 2015 was approximately USD 8,000. According to the criteria on the category of national development stage released by the WB in 2013, China shall be categorized as the country of medium to high income and shows a gap of about USD 5,000 to the threshold of high-income countries of USD 12,616. Based on the annual growth rate of per-capita GDP in China in recent years and the gradual increase of the threshold of high-income countries, it still takes over a decade for China to join the rank of high-income countries. In this process, China still enjoys a great potential of development.

Therefore, according to general laws of evolution of the economic development stage, China still has a rapid-development period for at least 10 to 20 years before full realization of industrialization, urbanization and modernization. Currently, China is stepping into the new stage of deep integration, mutual coordination and simultaneous development of the new style of industrialization with Chinese characteristics, informatization, urbanization and agricultural modernization. The rapid economic development will be accompanied by transformation, upgrading and rationalization of the economic structure, which will promote concentrated outbreak of "advantages of backwardness" and realize the great-leap-forward economic development.

II. The great power advantage is the important support to Chinese economy

China is not only a developing country but also a developing big power, and it enjoys the great-power advantages that are not seen in general developing countries.

The first is the population advantage. Labor is the living source for all social wealth and the labor force is the primary factor for productivity. China has a population of 1.36 billion, including 902 million in labor age. In addition to the large population, the labor force in China ranks the top of the world in terms of the labor quality, like working hard and being quick in learning, which constitutes the fundamental factor for constant rapid economic development in China. Along with thorough implementation of the strategy of invigorating the country through science, technology and education, advancement of the new urbanization road and gradual fulfillment of reform in the household registration system, retirement system and fertility system, it will further liberate the labor, improve enthusiasm of laborers, increase the employment population and bring powerful driving force for economic development.

The second is the space advantage. The vast land, rich resources, regional variance and complete economic system in China give rise to the unique advantage of Chinese economy on space development. First, the scale economy generated based on the large-scale concentration of production factors promote constant improvement of the production efficiency. Second, the economy of scope emerging upon various types of products promotes expansion of the labor division. Third, the gradient effect due to regional variance promotes complementary advantages and coordinated development among the regions. The space advantage also creates the objective foundation for the great tenacity, potential and leeway for Chinese economy.

The third is the advantage on internal demands. Production determines exchange; labor division constitutes the foundation for the market economy, and the degree of labor division determines the depth and width of the market and thus decides the scale of the market. The great population and rich labor resources not only create the great production capability and the market supply but also generate the great exchange capability and the market demand, making the unlimited source that guarantees the great internal demands in China. As the report of the 18th Party Congress expressly pointed out "overall improvement of people's living standards" and "the goal to double the residents' income by 2020", the great demand on consumption exceeding tens of trillion Yuan will be released by then, which will lead to huge demand on investment.

The fourth is the advantage on capital accumulation. The capital accumulation is the key factor that promotes economic development, while the growth of investment accumulation is decided by the growth of savings. The average saving rate in China is 38.7% since 1978 and is steadily growing after entering the new century. According to analysis by the State Statistical Bureau, the saving rate in China reached 52% in 2012, which was unique in the world, and would maintain the trend in a relatively long period. Along with constantly deeper reform of the financial system, it would become smoother and more efficient to convert savings to investment, and the advantage on capital accumulation in China would become more remarkable.

After the World War II, some Asian countries and regions represented by the "Four Asian Tigers" had once attained the rapid growth lasting for 30 years, as is known as the "East Asia Miracle". Though China is an East Asian country and shares some similarities with other East Asian countries, its development logic is somewhat different to the so-called East Asia Miracle. For example, the great-power advantage is unique for China, in addition to the institutional advantage mentioned next. So, the Chinese miracle is different with the East Asia Miracle.

III.   The institutional advantage is the basic guarantee for Chinese economy

China is not only a developing big power but also a developing big socialist power, so it features the special institutional advantage which is unique in China – i.e., the institutional advantage on the socialist market economy.

With private ownership as its basis, the capitalist market economy necessarily gives rise to profound conflicts and defects such as class antagonism, economic crisis and polarization. As the general representative of the bourgeoisie, capitalist countries have to conduct direct and indirect intervention on the economy. However, the intervention in the economy by capitalist countries always faces the fundamental conflict due to restriction by private ownership that the too weak government intervention can hardly solve the severe issues coherent in the capitalist market economy including unemployment and economic crisis, etc., and the too strong government intervention will damage the principle of the sanctity of private ownership and the vitality of the capitalist economy. Interweaving of the market failure and the government failure is the inevitable consequence for the development of the basic capitalist conflicts. Therefore, the capitalist market economy is impossible to realize constant rapid economic development.

With a great difference, the socialist market economy combines the basic socialist system and the market economy and gives play to both advantages of the market economy and the superiority of the socialist system. Therefore, it features new characteristics and new advantages beyond the capitalist market economy.

The socialist market economy is built on the foundation of keeping public ownership as the mainstay of the economy and allowing diverse forms of ownership to develop side by side. The mainstay position of the public ownership, particularly the leading role of the state-owned economy, is favorable to maintaining stability of the macro-economy, supporting operation of the national economy, improving the capability of independent innovation and promoting the national strength of the economy, national defense, national cohesion and capability to cope with kinds of emergencies and major risks. When giving play to the leading role of the state-owned economy, we still unswervingly encourage, support and guide development of economies of non-public ownership and attempt to create the new pattern of equal competition of mutual promotion of diverse forms of ownership, which will support the growth, promote innovation, expand employment, increase tax income and improve vitality of the market economy.

The competent Party and government and effective market constitute outstanding manifestation of the institutional advantages of the socialist market economic system and the dual engines to promote economic development. To enable the effective market, it is necessary to give full play to advantages of the market system including information sensitivity, high efficiency, effective excitation and flexible adjustment, etc., and promote vitality and efficiency of economic development. The competent Party and government is the fundamental characteristic of the socialist system in Chinese characteristics. In the socialist market economy, the government not only formulates market rules and controls the macro-economy but also serves as the general representative of the people's ownership of means of production and social public interests, so it is capable of controlling economic operation by gathering more resources, combining demands on economic and social development rationally with social financial and material resources and guiding the development of the national economy along the correct direction from aspects of planning, overall coordination, market regulation, management of state-owned assets and industrial policies, etc. In particular, the Party's capability in overall arrangement, coordination among all parties and driving the socialist market economy makes up the fundamental guarantee for the healthy development of the socialist market economy.

The Opening Up constitutes an important factor contributing to economic development in China since Reform and Opening Up. Deeper development of opening up helps acquire more external funds especially direct investment by multinational companies, relieves the issue of capital shortage during economic development, gives full play to the comparative advantages, explore the international market, relieves the issue on limited domestic market demands in economic development, introduce and learn from advanced technologies and management experiences overseas, exerts the advantage of backwardness, realizes technology leapfrogging, develops and improves the market economic system, intensify the fierceness of market competition and promote the efficiency of the economic system. Meanwhile, during the Opening Up, we adhere to the principle of independence, apply the gradual and controllable opening-up strategy, plan the domestic and foreign markets and resources as a whole, emphasize maintaining the national sovereignty and economic security, attempt to prevent and relieve the shock by international risks, maintain the control over key industries and areas and improve capability of independent innovation.

Give full play to the enthusiasm of the central and the local governments. As the center of social economy, politics and culture, the central government represents the overall and long-term interests of the whole country, safeguards the economic and political order of the society and plays as the leading power to promote economic development, economic Reform and Opening Up. Local governments are responsible to solely cope with local affairs under the scope of function stipulated by the Constitution and the institution, formulate the economic and social development of the region, coordinate the important economic relations of the area, maintain the market order, provide public services, drive market cultivation and promote economic and social development of the region. The centralization and the decentralization complement, cooperate with and restrict each other and jointly promote the economic and social development.

Institutional advantages of the socialist market economy are also manifested in many other aspects, including combining active participation in globalization and independence and making full use of domestic and international markets and resources, combining centralization and decentralization, giving full play to the enthusiasm of central and local government and combining efficiency and equality to enable all people enjoy the results of reform and development, etc.

The Third Plenary Session of the 18th Central Committee of the CPC has formulated the new strategy on deepening reform in an all-around way, and the new round of economic system reform is under progress. The success of the new round of reform will make the socialist market economic system more mature, stable and perfect and will render strong driving force for realization of constant rapid economic development.

IV. Economic development ushers in new normal

Since the international financial crisis in 2008, Chinese economy has been exposed some new important features such as changes to the speed, structure and driving force and ushered in the new normal for economic development. In this new normal, economic development in China presents the following characteristics: the growth rate changes from the high speed to the medium-high speed, the development method changes from the scale and speed orientation to the quality and efficiency orientation, the economic structure changes the main form of incremental expansion to adjusting the stock and optimizing the incremental and the driving force for development transfers from resources and low-cost labor to innovation. These changes make up the necessary process for the Chinese economy to develop to the stage of more advanced form, more optimum labor division and more rational structure. However, it is not easy to realize the wide and profound changes like these and constitutes a new big challenge for us.[1]

(1) Change to the growth rate

After 2012, the Chinese economy has changed from the high-speed growth around 10% to the medium-high-speed growth around 7%, which reflects the objective trend of economic growth as well as the new orientation for the macro-control in China.

Based on the objective trend of economic operation, the world economy sees constant weak growth, international market demands are fatigued, growth of demands on investment and consumption in China is slowing down, and the issue of overcapacity is prominent. Along with increasing restrictions by resources, ecology and environment and rising cost of labors, etc., it is difficult to continue the high growth rate based on high investment, high consumption and quantity expansion.

In terms of the orientation of the macro-control, as the development method changes from the scale and speed orientation to the quality and efficiency orientation in the new normal, the goal of the macro-control is to adapt to the change,

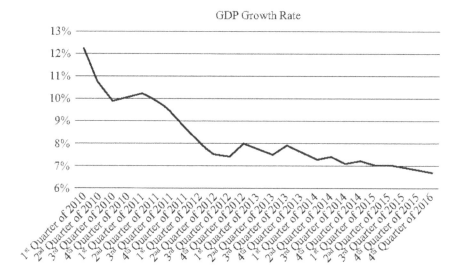

Figure 7.1

focus on sustainable growth with good quality and efficiency without exaggeration and realize economic growth by changing the method of economic development, optimizing the economic structure, improving the ecology and environment and improving the development quality and efficiency.

The Fifth Session of the 18th Central Committee proposed the goal to double the GDP and urban and rural residents' per-capita income by 2020 compared with 2010. To realize the goal, the annual economic growth between 2016 and 2020 must keep above 6.5%, so the task of building a well-being society in an all-around way can be completed as scheduled. China is now equipped with sufficient conditions to realize the goal, as it is still in the period of important strategic opportunities, features favorable material foundation, rich human resources, broad market and huge market potential ad sees no change in the basic tendency of long-term development.

(2) Optimization of the economic structure

After ushering in the new normal of economic development, the optimization of the economic structure in China is facilitated. Regarding the demand structure, the consumption demand is playing an increasingly important role in economic growth. In particular, after 2013, the contribution rate of consumption has seen significant growth, having increased from 50% in 2013 to 60% in the first half of 2015. At the same time, new commercial opportunities are constantly emerging along with wide development of personalized, diversified and quality-oriented consumption and online shopping and customized consumption as well as gradual consumption upgrading in service consumption, information consumption, green consumption, fashion consumption, quality consumption and rural area consumption, etc.

In terms of the industrial structure, the proportion of the service industry occupied 49.5% of gross national product (GNP) in the first half of 2015. From 2011 to 2014, the annual growth rate of increase value of the equipment manufacturing and hi-tech industry, respectively, reach 13.2% and 11.7%, respectively, 2.7% and 1.2% higher than the increase value by large-scale industry. Meanwhile, the transformation and upgrading of the traditional industry are speeding up, with constant emergence of new industries and new business forms.

For the urban and rural structure, urbanization is under progress. The urbanization rate in 2014 reached 54.77% and the new urban population is about 20 million every year. For the regional structure, the middle and western area shows the great development potential, while Chongqing and Guizhou are leading other provinces in economic growth rate. Implementation of the overall strategy for regional development led by construction of "the Belt and Road", coordinated development of Beijing, Tianjin and Hebei Province and construction of Yangtze River economic belt, etc., is constantly exploring the new room for regional development.

The optimization of the economic structure is the necessary result when economic development in China reaches a certain degree. However, it shall be noted that the extensive mode of growth and structural conflict formed in years have not been fundamentally changed, and it costs a certain time to relieve the overcapacity and optimize and upgrade the economic structure. Therefore, it is necessary to constantly promote new industrialization, informatization, urbanization and agricultural modernization, facilitate optimization and upgrading of the economic structure and push forward the industry to step from the medium and lower end to the medium and higher end.

(3)   Change to the driving force for development

The direct factors that promote economic development consist of two areas: first, increase of investment of capitals, labors and production factors such as land, and second, improvement of the efficiency of allocation of production factors. The latter one mainly relies on technological innovation. It is the necessary trend of productivity development and an important manifestation of economic development to rely more on innovation compared to the reliance on factors input in previous time.

The capability in scientific and technological innovation in China has been constantly improving for years, even ranked among the top of the world in some important areas, and promoted China to transform from the role of "follower" to the role of "companion" and "leader". Innovation is constantly deepening in the industry, products, production method, industrial organization, business model and management system, etc. However, in general, Chinese economy is still big but not powerful and rapid but not optimum, lacks innovation capability and core technologies and faces increasingly greater pressure on the population, resources and environment and fewer material resources. Then as the old road is unpractical any longer, where is the new road? The new road is to rely more on innovation-driven development and rely more on technological innovation.

As the new round of technological revolution and industrial changes are rising, it brings forward great challenges to the development of China as well as the scarce historical opportunity for us to catch up developed countries. It is necessary to vigorously implement the strategy of innovation-driven development, attach more importance to technological innovation in important areas, carry out a batch of major technology programs related to the overall and long-term interests of the state and break the previous situation where the major core technologies are controlled by others in areas of strategic competition. Develop the new engine through innovation and create a new longer cycle of growth.

(4) Rise of the level of opening up

An opening-up pattern involving all aspects, broad area and multiple levels has been basically formed in over three decades since the Reform and Opening Up. By present, China has ranked number one in the world in terms of total import and export volume and absorption of foreign capitals. Meanwhile, it shall be noted that the Reform and Opening Up still has the room for improvement, such as the evident feature of rapid and deep opening up in coastal area and in the east and slow opening up in the inland and western area, low technical content and added value of exported products and only a few products of independent intellectual property and independent brand. Therefore, we are urged to facilitate optimization and upgrading of the Opening Up and realize the change to the driving force of growth and competitive advantages.

Along with the increasingly deepening economic globalization and profound reform of the global governance system, developing countries continue to accumulate power, international powers tend to be balanced, the coupling effect of domestic and international economy is becoming stronger, and China is becoming the advocator and builder of the world economic rules and order from the "accepter". This is an important change for the current Opening Up and is the necessary requirement due to the constantly rising position of China in the world economy. To promote the development of the Opening Up under this new condition, it is necessary to actively participate in global economic governance, push forward reform and improvement of the international economic governance system, actively lead the global economic agenda and urge the international economic order to develop in the equal and cooperative way.

(5) Dialectic between challenge and opportunity

The challenge and opportunity are the two sides of a coin, which is subject to mutual dependence and mutual transformation. When appropriately coping with the challenge, it becomes the opportunity, and when failing to seize the opportunity, it becomes the challenge. It requires conditions to transform the challenge to the opportunity or transform the opportunity to be challenged, relying on people's subjective initiative. As the economic development ushers in the new normal, the Chinese economy is encountered with many difficulties and challengers during operation, such as weak growth of investment, difficulty in production and operation of some enterprises, prominent issue of overcapacity, increasing financial risk and fatigued international market. However, if we are not restricted by the fluctuation of the economic growth rate in short term but look forward to the long-term tendency of economic development, we will know that these difficulties and challenges do not alter the judgment that China is still in the period of strategic opportunities. In the process of overcoming difficulties and coping with challenges, Chinese economy is stepping to the new stage and winning new opportunities, including integration and simultaneous development of new industrialization with Chinese characteristics; informatization, urbanization and agricultural modernization; improvement of innovation capability, as well as the deepening overall reform, rising levels of the Opening Up, optimizing industry and upgrading structure, increasing new growth points, expanding space pattern and providing room for expansion of domestic demands and so on. The new normal contains new opportunities and presents the new prospect. We shall comprehensively grasp opportunities, calmly cope with challenges, actively adapt to and lead the new normal of economic development, realize the historical leap of the Chinese economy from the big one to the strong one and usher in a brighter future of Chinese economy.

V. Attempt to realize shared development

How to further promote economic development in China under new historical conditions? According to the *Recommendations of Central Committee of the Communist Party of China for the 13th Five-Year Plan for Economic and Social Development* approved in the Fifth Plenary Session of the 18th Central Committee of CPC (hereinafter referred to as the *Recommendations*), a new strategy was proposed – i.e., firmly establishing the concept of innovative, coordinated, green, open and shared development, which is the scientific guideline for economic and social development in China under new circumstances. The five development concepts constitute an integral system, where shared development occupies the special and important position.

As is known to all, the social and economic development is a process of perfect integration of the productive forces and production relations, while the economic development in the socialist society also consists of two aspects: the productive forces and production relations, on the one hand, vigorously liberating and developing productive forces, constantly improving the labor productivity and creating more social wealth, and, on the other hand, constantly satisfying people's increasing demands on materials and culture, promoting all-around development of people and realizing common prosperity of all social members. The former one is the approach, while the latter one is the goal. The former is the requirement proposed by the development of productive forces, while the latter is the requirement of the socialist system. Only the perfect integration of the two sides could fully reflect essential characteristics of the socialist economic development – i.e., the people-centered shared development.

The differences between the socialism and the capitalism are manifested by many aspects, such as the ownership, distribution system, role of the state and political system. From the perspective of development, the difference lies in whether it is people centered or capital centered and whether it pursues the interests of the minority or the interests of the majority. These are two completely different development roads and development ideas.

The neoliberalism that has been popular in the capitalist world since the 1980s reflects the development centering on capitals and shows the essence to remove any obstacle that hinders the advancement of capitals, realize complete freedom of action of capitals and guarantee the maximum residual value by sacrificing the interests of laborers and the majority people of the society. The corresponding policies advocate worshiping private ownership and opposing public ownership, worshiping free market and opposing state control, worshiping market efficiency and opposing social equality, worshiping capital sovereignty and opposing labor sovereignty and worshiping unconditional opening up and opposing independence. Though the theories and policies of neoliberalism could stimulate the development of productive forces to a certain degree, they would necessarily lead to the polarization in wealth occupation, where the wealth is accumulated and expanded among a few people and most people are leading a relatively poorer life. It would finally result in class antagonism, economic crisis and anarchic state of production. The severe dangers of neoliberalism have been fully unveiled after the world financial and economic crisis in 2008, including the persistent depression of the world economy and increasingly intensified social chaos including developed capitalist countries, which warn people that the development road centering on capitals has no future.

It is the fundamental principle of scientific socialism and consistent position of the Communist Party of China to realize people-centered shared development. In the socialist society, along with the establishment of public ownership of means of production and the elimination of class antagonism, all social members become the co-owners of means of production, while the development of productive forces is not applied as the measure for the minority to exploiting the majority people but applied to satisfy materials demands of social members.

It is necessary to comprehensively understand the connotation of shared development. As pointed out by the General Secretary Xi Jinping, to adhere to the idea of people-centered development, the key is to realize the concept of shared development and reflect the requirement of the gradual realization of common prosperity. First, the shared development is shared by all people. Shared development means that everyone instead of the minority or part of people shares the results of development. Second, sharing here refers to sharing in an all-around way. Shared development refers to sharing construction results of national economy, politics, culture, society and ecology and fully safeguarding people's legal rights and benefits in all aspects. Third, the sharing is based on common construction. Give full play to democracy, widely gather people's intelligence, stimulate people's forces to the maximum degree and create the vivid scene where everyone participates in construction, spares no effort and wins their own sense of achievement. Fourth, sharing here is in a gradual form. The shared development necessarily experiences a process from the lower level to the higher level and from imbalance to balance and shows differences despite the high level.

Sharing is the goal as well as the measure. As proved by both theories and practices, efficiency and equality are unified instead of being contradicted. Realization of shared development is favorable to mobilizing initiative, enthusiasm and creativity of all parties, promoting people's all-around development and quality, realizing social harmony and stability and expanding people's demands. On the contrary, the too wide gap in wealth occupation and income distribution is unfavorable for mobilizing initiative, enthusiasm and creativity of the masses; promoting people's all-around development and quality; realizing social harmony and stability; and expanding people's demands; it damages political democracy and social equality, intensifies social conflicts and contradictions, even leads to social chaos and then impedes constant and healthy economic development.

Currently, fulfillment of the concept of shared development shows strong pertinence and major practical significance. Since the Reform and Opening Up, China has seen the huge development of social productive forces and constantly improving living standards of people, but is also encountered with some issues that cannot be neglected. For example, some local governments or sectors only pursue after quantity of materials wealth and GDP but ignore development of education, medical care and social security undertakings; along with significant rise of the total income, the gap in wealth and income distribution is evidently widening and the Gini coefficient has maintained above 0.45 for 10 consecutive years, suggesting the increasingly intensified polarization; the gap between the urban and rural area in education, hygiene, employment and social security demands urgent solution; some enterprises blindly pursue maximum profits, damage workers' legal rights and benefits, produce counterfeit and shoddy products and damage resources and environment; illegal behaviors during system reform of stock transaction, real estate development and state-owned enterprises lead to prominent issue of "windfall profits"; some cadres transact exchange between power and money, turn public property into private property, damage public interests to earn private interests, conduct corruption and severely damage people's interests, etc. These issues seriously violate against the idea of people-centered development, do not satisfy requirements of shared development and are unfavorable for constant and healthy economic development.

The proposals of people-centered development and shared development are not abstract or mysterious concepts and shall be reflected in various links in socialist economic and social development and specific behaviors than being only theories. It shall be noted that under the socialist market economy, realization of the idea of shared development requires giving play to the decisive role of the market mechanism in resources allocation. However, the market economy regards the exchange of equal values among individuals as the basis, private interests as the driving force and spontaneity as the adjusting method. The spontaneous market economy necessarily leads to polarization of wealth and is impossible to guarantee equality and justice and realize the common prosperity and the goal. Therefore, in addition to giving full play to the role of the market mechanism, it is necessary to give better play to the Party leadership and the role of government, better reflect the dominant role of people and better exert the superiority of the socialist system. Ultimately, we shall build the more mature socialist economic system and institutional system with Chinese characteristics, better combine the basic socialist system and the market economy and fulfill the idea of people-centered development and shared development.

Firmly adhere to the center of economic construction, vigorously develop social productive forces, improve the quality and efficiency of economic development and produce more and better material and spiritual products and constantly meet people's increasing demands on materials and culture.

Comprehensively mobilize people's enthusiasm, initiative and creativity, create the stage and environment to enable laborers, entrepreneurs and innovative talents from all industries and sectors and cadres at all levels to exert their role and fully stimulate social vitality and creativity.

Develop people's democracy, safeguard social equality and justice, assure people's rights in equal participation and equal development, particularly carry forward economic democracy and fulfill the principle of people being the master in all areas and aspects of national economic management.

Adhere to improving the basic socialist economic system, unswervingly consolidate and develop the public-owned economy and give better play to the major role of state-owned enterprises in safeguarding people's common interests. Unswervingly encourage, support and guide development of non-public-owned economy, establish harmonious labor relation in non-public ownership and incorporate them as the builder of the socialist undertakings with Chinese characteristics.

Adhere to the basic socialist distribution system. Adjust the pattern of income distribution; improve the re-distribution adjustment system with taxation, social security and transfer payment as major measures; maintain social equality and justice; solve the issue of the income gap; popularize the development results in an equal way to cover all people; and realize common prosperity of social members.

Adhere to safeguarding and improving people's living standards as the starting point and goal of economic development; comprehensively solve the issues on education, employment, income, social security, medical care and food safety concerns of the people; and popularize reform and development results among the masses in a more practical way.

Increase supply of public services, adhere to the direction of universal benefits, guarantee of the basic supply, equal supply and sustainable supply, start from solving the most direct and practical interest issue people concern the most, promote the government's responsibilities and improve the capability of common construction and sharing of public services.

Adhere to the strategy of giving priority to employment, carry out more active employment policies, create more employment positions and focus on solving the structural conflict of employment. Improve the policies on supporting the start-ups, drive employment with start-ups and build the start-up service platform for everyone.

Form the sustainable basic public service system covering both rural and urban area under guidance by the government, the fairer and more sustainable social security system and the safe, efficient, convenient and low-cost public hygiene and basic medical service system.

Improve people's living standards in a universal way, implement the poverty alleviation program, carry out targeted measures, promote the quality of basic education and medical service in poor areas and realize equal basic public services in poor areas.

Establish a sound institutional system and mechanism featuring industrially promoted agriculture, urban-driven rural area, mutual benefits between industry and agriculture and integration of urban and rural area, so as to enable the broad farmers to equally participate in the process of modernization and jointly share results of modernization.

VI. Scientifically understand the "middle-income trap"

The so-called middle-income trap was first proposed by the WB in the *Report on East Asian Economic Development* in 2006. It means that after the per-capita income attains USD 3,000, emerging economies suffer a concentrated outbreak of various conflicts accumulated in rapid development and cannot join the rank of high-income countries due to long-term stagnation of the economy. Through over three decades of rapid development, the per-capita national income in China reached USD 4,240 in 2010 and approached USD 8,000 in 2014 and China is now exposed to the transition from the middle income to high income. Therefore, many scholars believe that the economic development in China will face a series of severe conflicts and challengers, and may fall in the "middle-income trap". How to get cross the "middle-income trap" has currently become the hot topic that draws wide attention in the academic circle and the whole society. In view of this, it is necessary to apply the Marxist ideas to conduct in-depth research on this issue and reach scientific understanding.

First, it shall be noted that the so-called middle-income trap is not a universal law. According to the latest criteria on categorization issued by the WB in 2015, the countries with the per-capita national income ranging between USD 1,045 and USD 12,746 in 2013 all belong to middle-income countries. (The WB refers to the per-capita gross national income to revise the category of world economic entities every year. The criteria have been constantly increasing due to inflation of prices and some other factors.) Along with the development of the world economy, the quantity of high-income countries is ceaselessly increasing. By now, there are 75 high-income countries (with the per-capita national income higher or equal to USD 12,746 in 2013), 105 middle-income countries and 34 low-income countries in the world. In comparison, in 1996, based on the criteria of the WB, the quantity of high-income countries (or regions) was 45 (with the per-capita national income higher than or equal to USD 8,956 in 1994), which was increased to 50 in 2001 (with the per-capita national income higher than or equal to USD 9.266 in 1999) and to 55 in 2005 (with the per-capita national income higher than or equal to USD 9,386 in 2003). Based on conditions in recent years, some countries called the representative of "middle-income trap", such as Malaysia, Argentina, Brazil, Chile and Mexico, have maintained rapid growth rate, with the per-capita income approaching to or exceeding USD 10,000, and are about to step into the rank of high-income countries. On the contrary, after the international financial crisis in 2008, some developed countries have been suffering the so-called new normal – i.e., constantly rising unemployment rate, economic downturn and intensified polarization, and fallen into the so-called high-income trap. It can be seen that the so-called middle-income trap is not the universal fact or general law.

Second, it shall be seen that the countries falling into the so-called middle-income trap are encountered with complicated problems under specific historical conditions and show no direct and necessary relationship with the so-called middle income. The per-capita income is only a concept of statistical significance but does not reflect any economic law. As said by Friedrich Engels, "conditions for production and exchange by people vary in different countries and vary in different generations in every country. Therefore, the political economics is not the same in different countries and different historical conditions". For another example, as calculated based on the current price of US dollars, it was the late 1880s when the per-capita income in America reached USD 3,000, compared to the end of 19th century and the beginning of the 20th century for Argentina and 2008 for China. Conditions are completely different, and cannot be compared. In the current world, more than 100 countries ranking at the middle-income level show great differences in terms of development stage, social institution, economic system, resources endowments and cultural tradition, and are facing different issues, which can hardly be explained with a vague and general concept of middle-income trap; otherwise, it would ignore the particularity of conflicts and fall into the quagmire of metaphysics.

Third, it shall be emphasized that China, as a socialist power with vast land, large population and long tradition under development and transition, is experiencing the interweaved historical changes including deep integration and simultaneous development of industrialization, informatization, urbanization and agricultural modernization, as well as marketization, globalization and reform of the socialist institution, and China features the rarely complicated, rich and particular road of economic development and the incomparable historical advantages, big power advantages and institutional advantages. Therefore, if comparing the issues encountered by the Chinese economy at the current stage with other middle-income countries such as Malaysia, Philippines and Thailand, etc., and listing China and these countries as the major object that may fall into the "middle-income trap", despite the warning function for China, it has no significance since it is comparing a cat to a tiger and cannot clarify the periodic characteristics for economic development in China and accurately master conflicts and issues that emerge in Chinese economy and society.

Fourth, we shall see through the appearance to perceive the essence. Therefore, the key factor that decides the development level of a state is not the per-capita income, but the productive capability especially the technological innovation, and the key actor that decides the living quality of people is not the average income but the rational distribution of income. The symptoms of so-called middle-income trap such as economic stagnation, political upheaval, difficulty in employment, lack of innovative capability and fragile financial system are fundamentally related to the underdeveloped productive forces, backward production relations and weak state strength instead of the middle income. After the Industrial Revolution, western countries had led to realize modernization and acquired the dominating role in the international relation. At the end of the 19th century and beginning of the 20th century, developed capitalist countries in Europe and America stepped into the stage of imperialism, while backward countries became the colonial or semi-colonial land to developed countries, which formed the capitalist world system characterized by separation and contradiction between the developed and underdeveloped countries or between the center and the periphery. As stated by Vladimir Lenin, "The capitalism has become the world system where the very few 'advanced' countries imposing colonial oppression and financial strangulation over the majority residents of the world". In this system, most countries are locked in the underdeveloped status, except for a few countries (such as Japan and South Korea), and cannot attain the rank of developed countries. The so-called middle-income trap is only a manifestation of the underdevelopment.

Why are the most developing countries restricted to the underdeveloped status? The fundamental source is the capitalist world system itself. In the capitalist world system, everyone is born unequal, demonstrated by the capital's dominance over the labor and polarization of the wealth occupation within a country and the dominance of a few developed countries over the most underdeveloped countries and polarization of the wealth occupation between countries. Developed countries are playing the dominant role in the economy, politics, culture, military, science and technology and control over strategic resources, while the underdeveloped countries are subject to the dominance and see "reliance" on developed countries. The general law of the evolution of this unequal system is that the poor will become poorer and the rich will become richer, and the stronger will always be strong and the weaker will always be weak. This is the specific manifestation of general laws about capital accumulation unveiled by Karl Marx in international economic relations.

In view of internal conditions of underdeveloped countries, the relative backward productive forces and production relations put them at the marginal status in the world capitalist system under special difficulties in economic and social development. When analyzing the issue of Germany, Karl Marx once pointed out, "Same with all other countries in the Western Europe, we suffer from the development of the capitalist production as well as underdevelopment of the capitalist production in all other aspects". Not only being applicable to the conditions of Germany in the early 19th century, this statement of Karl Marx also enlightens our profound understanding about the "middle-income trap". "Suffering from underdevelopment of the capitalist production" means that many residues from the old society still exist in transition of developing countries from the traditional society to the capitalist society, such as natural economy, separation of the rural and urban area, autocratic monarchy, unification of the state and the religion and legal relaxation, which impede the modernization of the state. "Suffering from development of the capitalist production" means that defects of modern capitalism are increasingly intensified such as the contradiction between labor and capital, polarization between the poor and the rich and economic crisis along with a break-down of the traditional society and development of the capitalist institution. The economic and social development would necessarily fall into the trap of long-term stagnation and chaos due to sufferings from both of the development and under-development of the capitalist production, control by developed countries for the long term and loss of capability in independent development.

In conclusion, the so-called middle-income trap is only a phenomenon, while its essence is about how to get rid of poverty and passive position in the capitalist world system, improve the state capability in independent development, narrow the gap with developed countries and realize economic and social moderniza-tion. In this sense, it is not a new issue, but the subject of democratic revolution and socialist revolution in China in modern times, as well as the subject of the socialist construction and reform and the Opening Up. Under the leadership of the Communist Party of China and upon arduous exploration, efforts and struggles by Chinese people in the long term, China has found a correct road to realize modernization and go beyond the "middle-income trap" and achieved great suc-cess. The fundamental reason for the success lies in adhering to, improving and innovating the social system and development road selected by Chinese people; adhering to the road of common prosperity; formulating the basic national strategy of promoting independent innovation capability; and fulfilling the strategy at all aspects of modernization construction and winning the initiative of development by actively joining the economic globalization and fierce international competi-tion and leading the world as the front rank. At the current stage, it is necessary to actively adapt to and guide the new normal of economic development; facilitate transformation of the economic development method; accelerate construction of the innovation-oriented country; promote the transition from "made in China" to "created by China", from Chinese speed to Chinese quality and from Chinese products to Chinese brand; build the open, independent, complete and powerful scientific and technological system, industrial system, trade system, financial sys-tem, fiscal system and national governance system based on the foundation; and realize the historical leap from the economic giant to the economic power.

Note

1 Xi Jinping, "Speech on the Opening Ceremony for Seminar for Major Leaders and Cad-res at the Provincial and Departmental Level to Study Fulfillment of the Spirit of the Fifth Session of the 18th Central Committee", *People's Daily*, May 10, 2016.

Index

Page numbers in bold indicate a table on the corresponding page.

middle-income trap: categorization 156–157; manifestation of underdevelopment 158–159; role of political economics in 157; *see also* Chinese current economic development considerations
mixed-ownership structure 59–60; *see also* socialist market economy
M structure 28, 95, 102
Myrdal, Gunnar 12

National Congress: 12th 49, 69, 126; 13th 50, 69, 126; 14th 50, 53, 69, 126; 15th 79; 17th 29, 50, 54, 137; 18th 29–30, 39, 50, 145
neoclassical economics 12, 15–18, 26–27, 67, 86–87
neoliberal economics 12–14, 27, 39, 56, 77, 153
New China 1, 31, 32, 38, 49, 143

On the Ten Major Relationships 1
opening up characteristics 35–36; *see also* Chinese economic model analysis
out-system reforms 93–94; *see also* gradual reform considerations

people-centered development 153–156; *see also* Chinese current economic development considerations
people-oriented economic development 58–59; *see also* socialist market economy
planned arrangement 135; *see also* government/market interactions in socialist market economy
political economics: Chinese economic model analysis 24–45; economic reform, practices of 2–4, 16, 17, 21; gradual reform considerations 99–102; income distribution 25, 34; Marxism 5–10
population advantage 145; *see also* Chinese current economic development considerations
privatization: as examined in different economies 119–120; industry 111–114; as a neoliberal policy 39–40, 61; as part of radical reform 26–28, 77, 79, 86, 93–95
public service 135–136; *see also* government/market interactions in socialist market economy

Qian Yingyi 28, 95, 102

radical reform 76–106; initial condition disadvantages 103; macro-economic policy consequences 90–92
Reform and Opening Up *see* economic reform, practices of; gradual reform considerations; socialist market economy
resource allocation 66–67; *see also* socialist market economy
Ricardo, David 16, 20; *see also* Smith, Adam
Role of Reform and Planning in the 1990s 22, 102

Sachs, Jeffrey 26, 102, 103, 119
Samuel, Huntington 45
savings rate advantage 145; *see also* Chinese current economic development considerations
Schumpeter, Joseph 21
scientific socialism 5, 8–9, 20, 51–53; connotation of socialism 51; innovation 51–52, 137; market economy evolution 52–53; *see also* Marxism; socialist market economy
shared development concept, promotion of 152–156; people-centered development 153–156; sharing as a goal and measure 153–154; socialism *vs.* capitalism 153
shock treatment *see* radical reform
Smith, Adam 16, 17, 20, 27
socialism *see* socialist market economy
socialist market economy: addressing popular misconceptions 131–133; Chinese economic model analysis 33–34, 36–38, 76–106; contract economy considerations 70–71; defects of capitalism 7, 54–57, 63–64; definitions 3; economic democracy considerations 63–65; economic globalization considerations 62–63; economic reform, practices of 1–22, 49–74; evolutionary capacity 69–70; exchange economy considerations 70–71; government/market interactions 126–142; income distribution 59, 60, 65, 68, 137–138, 141; institutional advantage 58–65, 146–148; integration into market economy 72–74; introduction in China 49–51; labor-oriented distribution system 60–61; macro-function state *vs.* micro-efficient private 114–116, 136, 138–140; marketization reform 71;

For Product Safety Concerns and Information please contact our EU
representative GPSR@taylorandfrancis.com
Taylor & Francis Verlag GmbH, Kaufingerstraße 24, 80331 München, Germany

www.ingramcontent.com/pod-product-compliance
Ingram Content Group UK Ltd.
Pitfield, Milton Keynes, MK11 3LW, UK
UKHW020948180425
457613UK00019B/585